20 YEARS OF INTERNET HUMOR

Volume Three

Finding Wisdom, Warmth, and Laughter in a Changing Digital World

COMPILED BY

W.G. WILLIAMS

Published by WGWILLIAMS LLC LTD
Perrysburg, Ohio

IBSN 979-8-9935622-2-3 (Paperback)
IBSN 979-8-9935622-3-0 (Digital)

Printed in the United States of America

Contents

Acknowledgements

Well, if **Volume One** was my introduction to the hybrid publishing world, **Volume Two** got me started into another new world, that of independent publishing … and yes, there was a big difference. And a huge new learning curve.

First of all, I have to give a big shout out to all the readers of my daily emails. They have been VERY supportive and daily send me their comments about recent "Thoughts" as well as contributions for future use. Without their support and encouragement, I would never have gotten this far. Thank you all!

Now, to the help I received in this independent publishing world … dealing with formatting and the intricacies of getting stuff from my laptop to KDP has also been a new experience. I have had to lean heavily on the expertise of **Nick Caya** and **Kate Henderson** of **Word-2-Kindle** to keep me on the right track.

Keeping my website current is another thing totally out of my experience and I've been able to count on **Kristina Velpel**, my website manager at **ZING**, to keep my website current and running smoothly.

I can't overlook **Steve Henderson** at **Bradley Communications** who actually got me started on this road. He's still been involved along with **Cristina Smith**, **Kim Cruse**, and **Amy Collins** on his great staff.

But let's not overlook the covers! I stumbled onto a really GREAT graphic artist, **Kerri Brimmer** of **Brimming Design** in Rossford, Ohio. Kerri is a marvel. I can call her with an idea and seemingly within an hour I have proposals in my computer. My hardest job is to choose among several that are ALL good!

And of course, all the folks who have contributed "Thoughts" over the years. This volume has a number of new contributors including **Gary Abke, Raul Ascunce, Bill D'Antonio, Jim Greenwood, Jim Haile, Dawn Heisler, David Hoiles, Donald O'Dell, Steve Overholt, Debby Papay, Les Skinner, Wells Teague,** and **Barbara Wonderly.** By "new" contributors, I mean new to these printed tomes. Some of their contributions are as many as 20 years old. To be counted among this distinguished group you actually have to have sent me something you think I can use.

Most of my thanks has to go to my family, my wife **Jean** and my daughters **Carrie** and **Erin**, who put up with my seemingly endless hours at the computer editing the daily "Thoughts" and putting these volumes together. I REALLY appreciate their forbearance and silent support.

Introduction

Riding the Waves of Absurdity

Welcome back to the wild and wonderful world of internet humor! If Volume One was our comical launching pad and Volume Two took us deeper into the chaotic depts of online laughs, then this third volume is our exhilarating surf ride on the ever-changing tides of digital hilarity.

Over the last decade we've witnessed an explosion of creativity that defies classification – meme culture has morphed and evolved, birthed from the fertile ground of social media and collective imagination. Just when you think you've seen it all, the internet conjures up new gems that make you laugh, cringe, and sometimes scratch your head in confusion.

In this volume, we dive into the heart of the absurd, celebrating memes that went viral, the spontaneous moments that sparked joy, and the digital phenomena that defined online culture. From the triumphant to the trivial, it's a collection of the bizarre highlights and undercurrents that show just how wonderfully unpredictable humor can be in our interconnected lives.

What's startling is how these snippets of humor transcend time and trend – each joke, each meme carries a piece of our collective experience, permanently etched in the annals of the internet. And while some may argue that the best days of internet humor are behind us, I'm here to assure you that the laughter has only evolved.

This is not merely a compilation of popular jokes and inspirational stories – some entries may puzzle, some might evoke nostalgia, and others may strike a nerve. However, they all share a common thread: they are expressions of human creativity and connection, served with a side of absurdity that only the internet can provide.

So, let's embark on this journey together — a celebration of the memes, the madness, and the moments that kept the spirit of humor alive amidst the chaos of this digital age. Each page invites you to lose yourself in a world of laughter, where the punchlines are as versatile as the people who created them.

Thank you for joining me once again. Strap in because this ride promises to be a delightful whirlwind of the unexpected.

--Bill Williams

25 Things I Learned from My Mother

9/14/2006

1. **<u>My mother taught me TO APPRECIATE A JOB WELL DONE</u>**.
"If you're going to kill each other, do it outside. I just finished cleaning."

2. **<u>My mother taught me RELIGION</u>**.
"You better pray that will come out of the carpet."

3. **<u>My mother taught me about TIME TRAVEL</u>**.
"If you don't straighten up, I'm going to knock you into the middle of next week!"

4. **<u>My mother taught me LOGIC</u>**.
" Because I said so, that's why."

5. **<u>My mother taught me MORE LOGIC</u>**.
"If you fall out of that swing and break your neck, you're not going to the store with me."

6. **<u>My mother taught me FORESIGHT</u>**.
"Make sure you wear clean underwear, in case you're in an accident."

7. **<u>My mother taught me IRONY</u>**
"Keep crying, and I'll give you something to cry about."

8. **<u>My mother taught me about the science of OSMOSIS</u>**.
"Shut your mouth and eat your supper."

9. <u>My mother taught me about CONTORTIONISM</u>.
"Will you look at that dirt on the back of your neck!"

10. <u>My mother taught me about STAMINA</u>.
"You'll sit there until all that spinach is gone."

11. <u>My mother taught me about WEATHER</u>.
"This room of yours looks as if a tornado went through it."

12. <u>My mother taught me about HYPOCRISY</u>.
"If I told you once, I've told you a million times. Don't exaggerate!"

13. <u>My mother taught me the CIRCLE OF LIFE</u>.
"I brought you into this world, and I can take you out."

14. <u>My mother taught me about BEHAVIOR MODIFICATION</u>.
"Stop acting like your father!"

15. <u>My mother taught me about ENVY</u>.
"There are millions of less fortunate children in this world who don't
    have wonderful parents like you do."

16. <u>My mother taught me about ANTICIPATION</u>.
"Just wait until we get home."

17. <u>My mother taught me about RECEIVING</u>.
"You are going to get it when you get home!"

18. <u>My mother taught me MEDICAL SCIENCE</u>.
"If you don't stop crossing your eyes, they are going to freeze that way."

19. <u>My mother taught me ESP</u>.
"Put your sweater on; don't you think I know when you are cold?"

20. **<u>My mother taught me HUMOR</u>**.
"When that lawn mower cuts off your toes, don't come running to me."

21. **<u>My mother taught me HOW TO BECOME AN ADULT</u>**.
"If you don't eat your vegetables, you'll never grow up."

22. **<u>My mother taught me GENETICS.</u>**
"You're just like your father."

23. **<u>My mother taught me about my ROOTS</u>**.
"Shut that door behind you. Do you think you were born in a barn?"

24. **<u>My mother taught me WISDOM</u>**.
"When you get to be my age, you'll understand."

25. **<u>My mother taught me about JUSTICE</u>**
"One day you'll have kids, and I hope they turn out just like you!"

Contributed by Gary Abke

911 Calls

6/2/2009

Dispatcher: 9-1-1 What is your emergency?
Caller: I heard what sounded like gunshots coming from the brown
house on the corner.
Dispatcher: Do you have an address?
Caller: No, I have on a blouse and slacks, why?

>———<‹‹ ● ››——<

Dispatcher: 9-1-1 What is your emergency?
Caller: Someone broke into my house and took a bite out of my ham
and cheese sandwich.
Dispatcher: Excuse me?
Caller: I made a ham and cheese sandwich and left it on the kitchen
table and when I came back from the bathroom, someone had
taken a bite out of it.
Dispatcher: Was anything else taken?
Caller: No, but this has happened to me before and I'm sick and tired
of it!

>———<‹‹ ● ››——<

Dispatcher: 9-1-1 What is the nature of your emergency?
Caller: I'm trying to reach nine eleven but my phone doesn't have an
eleven on it.
Dispatcher: This is nine eleven.
Caller: I thought you just said it was nine-one-one.

Dispatcher: Yes, ma'am nine-one-one and nine-eleven are the same thing.
Caller: Honey, I may be old, but I'm not stupid.

>———‹‹ ● ››~———‹

Dispatcher: 9-1-1 What's the nature of your emergency?
Caller: My wife is pregnant and her contractions are only two minutes apart.
Dispatcher: Is this her first child?
Caller: No, you idiot! This is her husband!

>———‹‹ ● ››>———‹

Dispatcher: 9-1-1
Caller: Yeah, I'm having trouble breathing. I'm all out of breath. Darn...I think I'm going to pass out.
Dispatcher: Sir, where are you calling from?
Caller: I'm at a pay phone. North and Foster.
Dispatcher: Sir, an ambulance is on the way. Are you an asthmatic?
Caller: No
Dispatcher: What were you doing before you started having trouble breathing?
Caller: Running from the Police.

Contributed by Linda Anderson

1919

2/20/2019

If you were around in 1919 and came upon the following poster

I mean,
seriously,

Wouldn't you just keep drinking?

Contributed by Tim Butler

A 5-year-old's First Job

11/28/2022

Here's a truly heartwarming story about the bond formed between a little 5-year-old girl and some construction workers that will make you believe that we all can make a difference when we give a child the gift of our time.

A young family moved into a house next to a vacant lot. One day, a construction crew turned up to start building a house on the empty lot.

The young family's 5-year-old daughter naturally took an interest in all the activity going on next door and spent much of each day observing the workers.

Eventually the construction crew, all of them "gems-in-the-rough," more-or-less adopted her as a kind of project mascot. They chatted with her, let her sit with them while they had coffee and lunch breaks, and gave her little jobs to do here and there to make her feel important.

At the end of the first week, they even presented her with a pay envelope containing ten dollars. The little girl took this home to her mother who suggested that she take the ten dollars "pay" she'd received to the bank the next day to start a savings account.

When the girl and her mom got to the bank, the teller was equally impressed and asked the little girl how she had come by her very own paycheck at such a young age. The little girl proudly replied, "I worked last week with a real construction crew building the new house next door to us."

"Oh, my goodness gracious," said the teller, "and will you be working on the house again this week, too?"

The little girl replied, "I will if those lazy SOBs at the lumber yard ever deliver the damn sheet rock."

Contributed by Ron Gargasz

A Dog's Tale

8/25/2009

They told me the big black Lab's name was Reggie as I looked at him lying in his pen. The shelter was clean, no-kill, and the people really friendly. I'd only been in the area for six months but everywhere I went in the small college town, people were welcoming and open. Everyone waves when you pass them on the street.

But something was still missing as I attempted to settle into my new life here, and I thought a dog couldn't hurt. Give me someone to talk to. And I had just seen Reggie's advertisement on the local news. The shelter said they had received numerous calls right after, but they said the people who had come down to see him just didn't look like "Lab people," whatever that meant. They must've thought I did.

But at first, I thought the shelter had misjudged me in giving me Reggie and his things, which consisted of a dog pad, bag of toys almost all of which were brand new tennis balls, his dishes, and a sealed letter from his previous owner.

Reggie and I didn't really hit it off when we got home. We struggled for two weeks (which is how long the shelter told me to give him to adjust to his new home). Maybe it was the fact that I was trying to adjust, too. Maybe we were too much alike.

For some reason, his stuff (except for the tennis balls - he wouldn't go anywhere without two stuffed in his mouth) got tossed in with all of my other unpacked boxes. I guess I didn't really think he'd need all his old stuff, that I'd get him new things once he settled in. But it became pretty clear pretty soon that he wasn't going to.

I tried the normal commands the shelter told me he knew, ones like "sit" and "stay" and "come" and "heel," and he'd follow them - when he felt like it. He never really seemed to listen when I called his name - sure, he'd look in my direction after the fourth of fifth time I said it, but then he'd just go back to doing whatever. When I'd ask again, you could almost see him sigh and then grudgingly obey.

This just wasn't going to work. He chewed a couple shoes and some unpacked boxes. I was a little too stern with him and he resented it, I could tell. The friction got so bad that I couldn't wait for the two weeks to be up, and when it was, I was in full-on search mode for my cell phone amid all of my unpacked stuff. I remembered leaving it on the stack of boxes for the guest room, but I also mumbled, rather cynically, that the "damn dog probably hid it on me."

Finally, I found it, but before I could punch up the shelter's number, I also found his pad and other toys from the shelter. I tossed the pad in Reggie's direction, and he snuffed it and wagged, some of the most enthusiasm I'd seen since bringing him home. But then I called, "Hey, Reggie, you like that? Come here and I'll give you a treat." Instead, he sort of glanced in my direction - maybe "glared" is more accurate - and then gave a discontented sigh and flopped down. With his back to me.

Well, that's not going to do it either, I thought. And I punched the shelter phone number. But I hung up when I saw the sealed envelope. I had completely forgotten about that, too. "Okay, Reggie," I said out loud, "let's see if your previous owner has any advice."

To Whoever Gets My Dog:

Well, I can't say that I'm happy you're reading this, a letter I told the shelter could only be opened by Reggie's new owner. I'm not even happy writing it. If you're reading this, it means I just got back from my last car ride with my Lab after dropping him off at the shelter. He knew something was different. I have packed up his pad and toys before and set them by the back door before a trip, but this time.. it's like he knew something was wrong. And something is wrong .. which is why I have to go to try to make it right.

So let me tell you about my Lab in the hopes that it will help you bond with him and he with you.

First, he loves tennis balls.. the more the merrier. Sometimes I think he's part squirrel, the way he hordes them. He usually always has two in his mouth, and he tries to get a third in there. Hasn't done it yet. Doesn't matter where you throw them, he'll bound after it, so be careful - really don't do it by any roads. I made that mistake once, and it almost cost him dearly.

Next, commands. Maybe the shelter staff already told you, but I'll go over them again: Reggie knows the obvious ones - "sit," "stay," "come," "heel." He knows hand signals: "back" to turn around and go back when you put your hand straight up; and "over" if you put your hand out right or left. "Shake" for shaking water off, and "paw" for a high-five. He does "down" when he feels like lying down - I bet you could work on that with him some more. He knows "ball" and "food" and "bone" and "treat" like nobody's business. I trained Reggie with small food treats. Nothing opens his ears like little pieces of hot dog.

Feeding schedule: twice a day, once about seven in the morning, and again at six in the evening. Regular store-bought stuff; the shelter has the brand.

He's up on his shots. Call the clinic on 9th Street and update his info with yours; they'll make sure to send you reminders for when he's due. Be forewarned: Reggie hates the vet. Good luck getting him in the car - I don't know how he knows when it's time to go to the vet, but he knows.

Finally, give him some time. I've never been married, so it's only been Reggie and me for his whole life. He's gone everywhere with me, so please include him on your daily car rides if you can. He sits well in the backseat, and he doesn't bark or complain. He just loves to be around people, and me most especially.

Which means that this transition is going to be hard, with him going to live with someone new.

And that's why I need to share one more bit of info with you .. His name's not Reggie. I don't know what made me do it, but when I dropped him off at the shelter, I told them his name was Reggie. He's a smart dog, he'll get used to it and will respond to it, of that I have no doubt. But I just couldn't bear to give them his real name. For me to do that, it seemed so final, that handing him over to the shelter was as good as me admitting that I'd never see him again. And if I end up coming back, getting him, and tearing up this letter, it means everything's fine. But if someone else is reading it, well .. well it means that his new owner should know his real name. It'll help you bond with him. Who knows, maybe you'll even notice a change in his demeanor if he's been giving you problems.

His real name is Tank. Because that's what I drive.

Again, if you're reading this and you're from the area, maybe my name has been on the news .. I told the shelter that they couldn't make "Reggie" available for adoption until they received word from my company commander. See, my parents are gone, I have no siblings, no one I could've left Tank with .. and it was my only real request of the Army upon my deployment to Iraq, that they make one phone call the shelter .. in the "event" .. to tell them that Tank could be put up for adoption. Luckily, my colonel is a dog guy, too, and he knew where my platoon was headed. He said he'd do it personally. And if you're reading this, then he made good on his word.

Well, this letter is getting to downright depressing, even though, frankly, I'm just writing it for my dog. I couldn't imagine if I was writing it for a wife and kids and family. But still, Tank has been my family for the last six years, almost as long as the Army has been my family. And now I hope and pray that you make him part of your family and that he will adjust and come to love you the same way he loved me.

That unconditional love from a dog is what I took with me to Iraq as an inspiration to do something selfless, to protect innocent people from those who would do terrible things .. and to keep those terrible people from coming over here. If I had to give up Tank in order to do it, I am glad to have done so. He was my example of service and of love. I hope I honored him by my service to my country and comrades.

All right, that's enough. I deploy this evening and have to drop this letter off at the shelter. I don't think I'll say another good-bye to Tank, though. I cried too much the first time. Maybe I'll peek in on him and see if he finally got that third tennis ball in his mouth.

Good luck with Tank. Give him a good home, and give him an extra kiss goodnight - every night - from me.

Thank you,
Paul Mallory

I folded the letter and slipped it back in the envelope. Sure, I had heard of Paul Mallory, everyone in town knew him, even new people like me. Local kid, killed in Iraq a few months ago and posthumously earning the Silver Star when he gave his life to save three buddies. Flags had been at half-mast all summer.

I leaned forward in my chair and rested my elbows on my knees, staring at the dog. "Hey, Tank," I said quietly.

The dog's head whipped up, his ears cocked and his eyes bright.

"C'mere boy."

He was instantly on his feet, his nails clicking on the hardwood floor. He sat in front of me, his head tilted, searching for the name he hadn't heard in months.

"Tank," I whispered. His tail swished. I kept whispering his name, over and over, and each time, his ears lowered, his eyes softened, and his posture relaxed as a wave of contentment just seemed to flood him. I stroked his ears, rubbed his shoulders, buried my face into his scruff and hugged him.

"It's me now, Tank, just you and me. Your old pal gave you to me." Tank reached up and licked my cheek. "So whatdaya say we play some ball? His ears perked again.

"Yeah? Ball? You like that? Ball?" Tank tore from my hands and disappeared in the next room.

And when he came back, he had three tennis balls in his mouth.

Contributed by Bubba & Bonnie Mehling

A Little Humor

6/22/2025

WHEN YOU'RE DEAD,
YOU DON'T KNOW
YOU'RE DEAD. THE PAIN
IS FELT BY OTHERS.

THE SAME THING
HAPPENS WHEN
YOU'RE STUPID.

A nurse walks into a bank,
exhausted after a 20 hour shift.
She pulls a rectal thermometer
out of her pocket and tries to
write a check with it.
She looks at the cashier and
says, "Well, that's just great!
Some asshole has got my pen!"

All of us older folks know all about living on the edge. We used to answer the phone without knowing who it was.

In 1980s I was riding my bike and fell off and hurt my knee. I'm telling you this now because we didn't have social media then

CABLE REPAIRMAN WAS ON THE STREET AND ASKED ME WHAT TIME IT WAS. I TOLD HIM BETWEEN 8AM AND 1PM.

YOU KNOW YOU'RE GETTING OLD WHEN YOU CAN'T WALK PAST A BATHROOM WITHOUT THINKING, "I MIGHT AS WELL PEE WHILE I'M HERE."

Being a little older,
I am very fortunate to
have someone call and
check on me everyday.
He is from India and is
very concerned about
my car warranty.

Ron Gargasz

A Look Back at 2009

1/5/2010

Let's drink to '09
with a good belt of wine
(though whiskey may well be more fitting!)
The recession was hairy,
the Swine Flu was scary,
and Oprah announced she was quitting!

While we loved Lady Gaga,
the Octomom saga
struck many as shameless and wrong.
We witnessed the rift
between Kanye and Swift,
and Phelps was caught smoking a bong!

When a pilot's quick brain
saved his passenger plane
on the Hudson, the tale was a thriller.
Balloon Boy was phony
as rubber baloney.
The abs on the werewolves were killer!

A governor's flame
was an Argentine dame,
bringing scandal to South Carolina.
There were pirate attacks,
there was Goldman and Sachs,
there was poisonous drywall from China!

The prez was sworn in
and he flashed us a grin
while exuding his usual charms.
Though some thought it shady,
the stylish First Lady
asserted her right to bare arms.

While Michelle was in Vogue,
Sarah Palin went Rogue,
and political tensions were showing.
With the gathering storm
over health care reform,
the Tea Party movement was growing.

The Hollywood crew
gave us "Transformers 2,"
while "Up" was a true work of art.
There was Brüno (a jerk!)
plus a young Captain Kirk
and an overweight mall cop named Blart.

Those admen on "Mad Men"
were sexy-yet-sad men
with lives full of pressure and toil.
Adam Lambert came out,
leaving no shred of doubt,
and who didn't love Susan Boyle?

O'Brien shone bright
as the star of "Tonight."
Stephanopoulos stepped in for Sawyer.
And of course a divorce
was so quickly in force
that we watched "Jon and Kate Plus Her Lawyer!"

When a huge SUV
  hit a hydrant and tree
    and the juiciest rumors proved true,
The endorsements went winging,
  for that kind of swinging
    just wasn't the Tiger we knew!

And Pop lost its King!
  What a terrible thing
    for an artist with hit after hit!
There were songs and orations
with loud lamentations,
for everyone knew This was It.

There were others as well
  who went out, sad to tell.
    We saw Cronkite and Kennedy fall.
Bea Arthur is gone,
Ed McMahon has passed on,
and Mary left Peter and Paul.

With the passing of Farrah
we ended an era
and Soupy and Swayze went too.
  DeLuise said goodbye,
    as did Oxy-Clean Guy
      and the soft-spoken star of "Kung Fu."

Yet some news was brighter
  and made us feel lighter
    in spite of our sorrows and peeves.
There was Google Wave chat
and a keyboarding cat.

There were trendy new blankets with sleeves!

Contributed by Julius Graw

A Real Sherlock Holmes

10/7/2025

From Facebook

The story is told of the time Sir Arthur Conan Doyle left a railway station in Paris and hailed a taxi. When a taxi pulled up, he got in and was about to tell the taxi driver where he wanted to go, when the driver asked, "Where can I take you Mr. Doyle?"

Doyle was surprised that the taxi driver recognized him and asked whether he knew him by sight.

"No sir! I've never seen you before."

Doyle was puzzled and asked what made him think he was Conan Doyle.

"This morning's paper," he said, "had a story about you being on vacation in Marseilles. This is the taxi stand to which people who return from Marseilles always come. Your skin color tells me you've been on vacation. The ink spot on your right index finger suggests to me that you're a writer. Your clothing is very English and not French. Adding up all those pieces of information, I deduced that you are Sir Arthur Conan Doyle."

"This is truly amazing," Doyle replied. "You're a real-life counterpart to my fictional creation, Sherlock Holmes."

"There IS one other thing," the driver said.

"What's that?" Doyle inquired

"Your name is on the front of your suitcase."

Contributed by Barbara Cowan

Ah, Romance

5/16/2006

<u>How to treat a woman:</u>
Wine her.
Dine her.
Call her.
Hold her.
Surprise her.
Compliment her.
Smile at her.
Listen to her.
Laugh with her.
Cry with her.
Romance her.
Encourage her.
Believe in her.
Pray with her.
Pray for her.
Cuddle with her.
Shop with her.
Give her jewelry.
Buy her flowers.
Hold her hand.
Write love letters to her.
Go to the ends of the earth and back again for her.

<u>How To Treat a Man</u>:
Show up naked.
Bring chicken wings.
Don't block the TV!!!

Contributed by David Taylor

The Airline Disaster

12/15/2006

Abe and Esther were flying to Australia for a two-week vacation to celebrate their 40th anniversary. Suddenly, over the public address system, the captain announced, "Ladies and gentlemen, I am afraid I have some very bad news. Our engines have ceased functioning, and we must attempt an emergency landing.

"Luckily, I see an uncharted island below us and we should be able to land on the beach. However, the odds are that we may never be rescued, and we'll have to live on the island for the rest of our lives!"

Thanks to the skill of the flight crew, the plane landed safely on the island. An hour later Abe turned to his wife and asked, "Esther, did we pay our $5,000 PBS pledge check yet?"

"No, sweetheart," she responded.

Abe, still shaken from the crash landing, then asked, "Esther, did we pay our American Express card yet?"

"Oh, no! I'm sorry. I forgot to send the check," she said.

"One last thing, Esther. Did you remember to send checks for the Visa and MasterCard this month?"

"Oy, forgive me, Abe," begged Esther. "I didn't send them, either."

Abe grabbed her and gave her the biggest kiss in 40 years.

Esther pulled away and asked, "What was that for?"

Abe answered, "Now I know they'll find us!"

Contributed by Ron Gargasz

Bad Timing

10/15/2009

Two guys were drinking in a bar. One said, "Did you know that lions have sex 10 to 15 times a night?"

"Damn," replied his friend, "and I just joined The Moose!"

W.G. Williams

Blonde Joke

7/13/1023

Two sisters, one blonde and one brunette, inherited the family ranch. Unfortunately, after just a few years, they were in financial trouble.

In order to keep the bank from repossessing their ranch, they needed to purchase a bull so that they could breed their own stock.

Upon leaving for the next state to check out a bull for sale, the brunette told her sister, "When I get there, if I decide to buy the bull, I'll contact you to drive out and bring it home."

The brunette arrived at the place that had the bull for sale, inspected the bull, and decided that she wanted to buy it. The owner told her that he will sell it for $599 … no less.

After paying him, she drove to the nearest town to send her sister a telegram to tell her the news. She walked into the telegraph office and said, "I want to send a telegram to my sister telling her that I've bought a bull for our ranch. I need her to hitch the trailer to our pickup truck and drive out here so we can haul it home."

The telegraph operator explained that he'll be glad to help her, and then added, it will cost 99 cents a word.

Well, after paying for the bull, the brunette realized that she'll only be able to send her sister one word.

After a few minutes of thinking, she nodded and said, "I want you to send her the word 'comfortable.'"

The operator shook his head. "How is she ever going to know that you want her to hitch the trailer to your pickup truck and drive out here to haul that bull back to your ranch if you send her just the word 'comfortable?'"

The brunette explained, "My sister's' blonde. The word is big. She'll read it very slowly. "Com-for-DA-bul."

Contributed by Sharon Buckholtz

Bob & Betty Hill

12/04/2008

Bob Hill and his new wife Betty were vacationing in Europe near Transylvania. They were driving in a rental car along a rather deserted highway. It was late and raining very hard and Bob could barely see 20 feet in front of the car.

Suddenly the car skidded out of control! Bob attempted to control the car, but to no avail! The car swerved and smashed into a tree.

Moments later, Bob shook his head to clear the fog. Dazed, he looked over at the passenger seat and saw his wife unconscious with her head bleeding! Despite the rain, the unfamiliar countryside, and his own injuries, Bob knew he had to carry her to the nearest phone.

Bob carefully picked his wife up and began trudging down the road. After a short while, he saw a light and headed towards it. It came from an old, large house. He approached the door and knocked.

A minute passed. A small, hunched man opened the door and Bob immediately blurted, "Hello, my name is Bob Hill and this is my wife Betty. We've been in a terrible accident and my wife has been seriously hurt. Can I please use your phone?"

"I'm sorry," replied the hunchback, "but we don't have a phone but my master is a doctor; come in and I will get him!"

As Bob brought his wife in, an elegant man came down the stairs. "I'm afraid my assistant may have misled you. I'm not a medical doctor; I'm a scientist. However, it's many miles to the nearest clinic and I've had basic medical training. I'll see what I can do. Igor, take them down to the laboratory."

With that, Igor picked Betty up and carried her downstairs with Bob following closely. Igor placed Betty on a table in the lab as Bob collapsed from exhaustion and his own injuries. Igor picked Bob up and placed him on an adjoining table.

After a brief examination, Igor's master looked worried. "Things are serious, Igor. Prepare a transfusion."

Igor and his master worked feverishly, but to no avail. Bob and Betty Hill were no more.

The Hills' deaths upset Igor's master greatly. Wearily, he climbed the steps to his conservatory which housed his grand piano. It was here that he had always found solace.

He began to play and a stirring, almost haunting, melody filled the house.

Meanwhile, Igor was still in the lab tidying up. His eyes caught movement and he noticed the fingers on Betty's hand twitch, keeping time to the haunting piano music.

Stunned, he watched as Bob's arm began to rise marking the beat! He was further amazed as Betty and Bob both sat straight up!

Unable to contain himself, he dashed up the stairs to the conservatory. He burst in and shouted, "Master, Master! ... The Hills are alive with the sound of music!"

Contributed by Bubba & Bonnie Mehling

The Bride's Mother's Dress

3/25/2011

Jennifer's wedding day was fast approaching. Nothing could dampen her excitement - not even her parents' nasty divorce.

Her mother had found the PERFECT dress to wear and would be the best-dressed mother-of-the-bride ever!

A week later, Jennifer was horrified to learn that her father's new young wife had bought the exact same dress as her mother!

Jennifer asked her father's new young wife to exchange it, but she refused. "Absolutely not! I look like a million bucks in this dress, and I'm wearing it," she replied.

Jennifer told her mother who graciously said, ''Never mind sweetheart. I'll get another dress. After all, it's your special day."

A few days later, they went shopping and did find another gorgeous dress for her mother.

When they stopped for lunch, Jennifer asked her mother, "Aren't you going to return the other dress? You really don't have another occasion where you could wear it."

Her mother just smiled and replied, "Of course I do, dear ... I'm wearing it to the rehearsal dinner the NIGHT BEFORE the wedding."

Contributed by David Taylor

A Bureaucratic Response

7/31/2007

The day I immigrated to the United States, I was given an alien ID card that featured a cute photo of me at age 15.

Years later, when I went to the courthouse to become a citizen, a clerk confiscated my card.

"What will you do with it?" my wife asked.

"We burn it" was the answer.

"Could you please cut the photo off and let us keep it?" my wife requested.

"Certainly not," said the clerk. "This card is official U.S. government property. As such it cannot be mutilated before it's destroyed."

Contributed by Tom Benner

Burma Shave Signs

9/7/2005

My "Thoughts" about our recent car trip made Gary Thornton think about the old Burma Shave signs. Remember those? In a time when we didn't have cd's or DVDs, kids played car games and watched for the next Burma Shave signs. Too bad kids today can't/won't experience them.

> Trains don't wander
> All over the map
> 'Cause nobody sits
> In the engineer's lap
> Burma Shave

> She kissed the hairbrush
> By mistake
> She thought it was
> Her husband Jake
> Burma Shave

For those who never saw the Burma Shave signs, here is a quick lesson in our history of the 1930s, '40's, and '50's. Before the Interstates when everyone had to drive on two lane roads, Burma Shave signs would be posted all over the countryside in farmers' fields.

They were small red signs with white letters. Five signs, about 100 feet apart, each containing one line of a four-line couplet with the fifth sign advertising Burma Shave, a popular shaving cream.

Here are more of the actual signs:

DON'T LOSE YOUR HEAD
TO GAIN A MINUTE
YOU NEED YOUR HEAD
YOUR BRAINS ARE IN IT
Burma Shave

DROVE TOO LONG
DRIVER SNOOZING
WHAT HAPPENED NEXT
IS NOT AMUSING
Burma Shave

BROTHER SPEEDER
LET'S REHEARSE
ALL TOGETHER
GOOD MORNING NURSE
Burma Shave

SPEED WAS HIGH
WEATHER WAS NOT
TIRES WERE THIN
X MARKS THE SPOT
Burma Shave

THE MIDNIGHT RIDE
OF PAUL FOR BEER
LED TO A WARMER
HEMISPHERE
Burma Shave

AROUND THE CURVE
LICKETY-SPLIT
ITS A BEAUTIFUL CAR
WASN'T IT?
Burma Shave

NO MATTER THE PRICE
NO MATTER HOW NEW
THE BEST SAFETY DEVICE
IN THE CAR IS YOU
Burma Shave

A GUY WHO DRIVES
A CAR WIDE OPEN
IS NOT THINKIN'
HE'S JUST HOPIN'
Burma Shave

AT INTERSECTIONS
LOOK EACH WAY
A HARP SOUNDS NICE
BUT ITS HARD TO PLAY
Burma Shave

BOTH HANDS ON THE WHEEL
EYES ON THE ROAD
THAT'S THE SKILLFUL
DRIVER'S CODE
Burma Shave

THE ONE WHO DRIVES
WHEN HE'S BEEN DRINKING
DEPENDS ON THE CAR
TO DO HIS THINKING
Burma Shave

CAR IN DITCH
DRIVER IN TREE
THE MOON WAS FULL
AND SO WAS HE.
Burma Shave

PASSING SCHOOL ZONE
TAKE IT SLOW
LET OUR LITTLE
SHAVERS GROW
Burma Shave

Deadly thoughts
About lights that shine
If he won't dim his
Then I won't dim mine
Burma Shave

And the all-time favorite:

Don't stick your arm
Out the window too far
It might go home
In another car
Burma Shave

Do these bring back memories? If not, you're too young!
If they do, you're older than dirt.
Have a great day! Stay young at heart!

Contributed by Gary Thornton

Can You Be a Frog?

1/10/2008

A six-year-old went to the hospital with his grandmother to visit his grandfather. When they got to the hospital, he ran ahead of his grandmother and burst into his grandfather's room. "Grandpa, Grandpa," he said excitedly, "as soon as Grandma comes into the room, make a noise like a frog!"

"What?" said his grandpa.

"Make a noise like a frog because I heard Grandma say to Momma that if you croak, we're going to Disney World!!!"

Contributed by Ron Gargasz

The Christmas Coat

12/19/2022

A man was fumblin' around one day
In a women's clothing store.
He'd found his wife a Christmas coat
And was headed for the door.

But he bumped into a little boy
Who looked like he was lost.
He said, "Mister can you help me
Find out how much something costs?

"Here it is almost Christmas
And the nights are gettin' cold
Wintertime is on us
And my mom don't have a coat.

I've been workin' for the neighbors
And saving for a time,"
And in his tiny, outstretched hand
Was a dollar and a dime.

His gaze went from that big-eyed boy
To that pretty Christmas coat
And he finally cleared away the lump
That had gathered in his throat.

He said "Son, that's just what this coat costs
We're lucky that we found 'er.'"
He turned around and gave a wink
To the lady at the counter.

She put it in a pretty box
And wrapped it up just so
And went off in the back
And found a big red Christmas bow.

He said "I thank you for your help, sir,
And I kindly thank you ma'am.
I hope y'all are gonna have a big Christmas.
Cause now I know I am."

Well, the old boy walked home busted
Except for the dollar and the dime
Thinkin' he'd just have to buy
The coat another time.

He told his wife that Christmas
This year wouldn't be much fun.
And he gently took her in his arms
And told her what he'd done.

She said, "Why you old softie,
I wouldn't trade you for a farm.
I've got two or three old coats
And your love to keep me warm."

She put that money in a matchbox
And placed it beneath their tree
And said, "That is the grandest gift
You've ever given me!"

The years went by like years will do
When people are in love.
Their marriage was a golden bond
That was forged by God above.

Then one day came some bitter news
That filled his heart with fright.
The doctor told the old man's wife
That she was going to lose her sight.

He said, "There's an operation we can do,
But it puts me on the spot
Cause it's a quite complex procedure
And it's going to cost a lot."

The old man said, "Doctor I'm a failure.
I've made no preparation.
We don't have the money
For that kind of an operation."

The doctor got the strangest look
And he sat there for a while
And then he slowly nodded
And he broke out in a smile.

He said, "Why sir, you can't fool me
You're a very wealthy man.
You long ago invested
In the world's best savings plan.

"I'll see she gets the best of care.
She's going to be just fine,
And the total cost to you old friend
Is a dollar and a dime."

The old man stared in disbelief
Then he recognized that smile…
The one he'd seen those years ago
On a loving thoughtful child.

He said, "What you gave to me that day
Was more than just a coat.
You gave me the gift of giving
And you gave my mother hope.

"My mother'd been mistreated,
Neglected and abused.
But she gave life just one more chance
And it was all because of you.

"Now every year she takes that coat
And lays it beneath our tree.
It represents to us the things
That Christmas ought to be.

"She says that when we leave this world
For a better home someday,
The only things that we'll take with us
Are the things we gave away."

Contributed by Dennis Bialecki

A Christmas Letter from God!

12/23/2005

To: My Children on Earth

From: GOD

Re: Idiotic religious rivalries

My Dear Children (and believe me, that's all of you),

I consider myself a pretty patient Guy. I mean, look at the Grand Canyon. It took millions of years to get it right. And how about evolution? Boy, nothing is slower than designing that whole Darwinian thing to take place, cell by cell and gene by gene. I've even been patient through your fashions, civilizations, wars, schemes, and the countless ways you take Me for granted until you get yourselves into big trouble again and again.

But on this occasion of My Son's birthday, I want to let you know about some things that are starting to tick me off.

First of all, your religious rivalries are driving Me up a wall. Enough already! Let's get one thing straight: These are your religions, not Mine. I'm the Whole Enchilada; I'm beyond them all. Every one of your religions claims there's only one of Me (which, by the way, is absolutely true). But in the very next breath, each religion claims it's My favorite one. And each claims its bible was written personally by me and that all the other bibles are man-made. Oh, Me. How do I even begin to put a stop to such complicated nonsense?

Okay, listen up now: I'm your Father and Mother, and I don't play favorites among My Children. Also, I hate to break it to you, but I don't write. My longhand is awful, and I've always been more of a "doer" anyway. So, all your books, including the bibles, were written by men and women. They were inspired, remarkable people, but they also made mistakes here and there. I made sure of that so that you would never trust a written word more than your own living Heart.

You see, one Human Being? -- even a Bum on the street -- is worth more than all the holy books in the world. That's just the kind of Guy I Am. My Spirit is not an historical thing. It's alive right here, right now, as fresh as your next breath.

Holy books and religious rites are sacred and powerful, but not more so than the least of You. They were only meant to steer you in the right direction, not to keep you arguing with each other, and certainly not to keep you from trusting your own personal connection with Me.

Which brings Me to My next point about your nonsense: You act like I need you and your religions to stick up for Me or "win souls" for My Sake. Please, don't do Me any favors. I can stand quite well on my own, thank you. I don't need you to defend Me, and I don't need constant credit. I just want you to be good to each other.

And another thing: I don't get all worked up over money or politics, so stop dragging My name into your dramas. For example, I swear to Me that I never threatened Oral Roberts. I never rode in any of Rajneesh's Rolls Royces. I never told Pat Robertson to run for president, and I've never ever had a conversation with Jim Bakker, Jerry Falwell, or Jimmy Swaggart! Of course, come Judgment Day, I certainly intend to.

The thing is, I want you to stop thinking of religion as some sort of loyalty pledge to Me. The true purpose of your religions is so that you can become more aware of Me, not the other way around. Believe Me, I know you already. I know what's in each of your hearts, and I love you with no strings attached. Lighten up and enjoy Me. That's what religion is best for.

What you seem to forget is how mysterious I Am. You look at the petty little differences in your scriptures and say, "Well, if this is the Truth, then that can't be!" But instead of trying to figure out My Paradoxes and Unfathomable Nature -- which, by the way, you never will -- why not open your hearts to the simple common threads in every religion?

You know what I'm talking about: love and respect everyone. Be kind. Even when life is scary or confusing, take courage and be of good cheer, for I Am always with you. Learn how to be quiet, so you can hear My Still, Small Voice (I don't like to shout). Leave the world a better place by living your life with dignity and gracefulness, for you are My Own Child. Hold back nothing from life, for the parts of you that can die will surely die, and the parts that can't, won't. So *don't worry, be happy.* (I stole that last line from Bobby McFerrin, but he stole it from Meher Baba in the first place.)

Simple stuff. Why do you keep making it so complicated? It's like you're always looking for an excuse to be upset. And I'm very tired of being your main excuse. Do you think I care whether you call me Yahweh, Jehovah, Allah, Wakantonka, Brahma, Father, Mother, or even The Void or Nirvana? Do you think I care which of My Special Children you feel closest to -- Jesus, Mary, Buddha, Krishna, Mohammed or any of the others? You can call Me and My Special Ones any name you choose, if only you would go about My business of loving one another as I love you. How can you keep neglecting something so simple?

I'm not telling you to abandon your religions. Enjoy your religions, honor them, learn from them, just as you should enjoy, honor, and learn from your parents. But do you walk around telling everyone that your parents are better than theirs? Your religion, like your parents, may always have the most special place in your heart; I don't mind that at all. And I don't want you to combine all the Great Traditions into One Big Mess. Each religion is unique for a reason. Each has a unique style so that people can find the best path for themselves.

But My Special Children -- the ones your religions revolve around -- all live in the same place (My Heart) and they get along perfectly, I assure you. The clergy must stop creating a myth of sibling rivalry where there is none.

My Blessed Children of Earth, the world has grown too small for your pervasive religious bigotry and confusion. The whole planet is connected by air travel, satellite dishes, telephones, fax machines, rock concerts, diseases, and mutual needs and concerns. Get with the program! If you really want to help Me celebrate the birthday of My Son Jesus, then commit yourselves to figuring out how to feed your hungry, clothe your naked, protect your abused, and shelter your poor. And just as importantly, make your own everyday life a shining example of kindness and good humor. I've given you all the resources you need, if only you abandon your fear of each other and begin living, loving, and laughing together.

Finally, My Children everywhere, remember whose birth is honored on December 25th, and the fearlessness with which He chose to live and die. As I love Him, so do I love each one of you. I'm not really ticked off, I just wanted to grab your attention because I hate to see you suffer. But I gave you Free Will, so what can I do now other than to try to influence you through reason, persuasion, and a little old-fashioned guilt and manipulation? After all, I Am the original Jewish Mother. I just want you to be happy, and I'll sit in The Dark. I really Am, indeed, I swear, with you always. Always. Trust In Me.

Your One and Only,

GOD

[Note: Bo Lozoff wrote this as an article for the *Human Kindness Foundation* newsletter at Christmas-time, 1989. It was then included in his 1990 book *Just Another Spiritual Book*.

[http://www.humankindness.org/godletter.html] Since then the essay has been widely circulated, though almost always uncredited. Radio commentator Paul Harvey included the piece in his radio program on two occasions, apparently receiving a deluge of calls, mail, and faxes (we hope mostly positive). Now this piece can be found at numerous websites, often edited, and usually listed as, "author unknown."]

Contributed by Richard Sandford

A Conservative's View of World History and Anthropology

4/7/2006

For centuries, humans existed as members of small bands of nomadic hunter/gatherers. They lived on deer in the mountains during the summer and would go to the coast and live on fish and lobster in winter.

The two most important events in all of history were the invention of the wheel, and the invention of beer. The wheel was invented to get man to the beer. These were the foundation of modern civilization and together were the catalyst for the splitting of humanity into two distinct subgroups: Liberals and Conservatives.

Once beer was discovered it required grain, and that was the beginning of agriculture. Neither the glass bottle nor aluminum can were invented yet, so while our early human ancestors were sitting around waiting for them to be invented, they just stayed close to the brewery. That's how villages were formed. Some men spent their days tracking and killing animals to B-B-Q at night while they were drinking beer. This was the beginning of what is known as "the Conservative movement."

Other men who were weaker and less skilled at hunting, learned to live off the conservatives by showing up for the nightly B-B-Q's and doing the sewing, fetching, and hair dressing. This was the beginning of the Liberal movement. Some of these liberal men eventually evolved into women. The rest became known as 'girliemen.'

Some noteworthy liberal achievements include the domestication of cats, the invention of group therapy and the concept of Democratic voting to decide how to divide the meat and beer that conservatives provided.

Over the years conservatives came to be symbolized by the largest, most powerful land animal on earth, the elephant. Liberals are symbolized by the jackass.

Modern liberals like imported beer (with lime added), but most prefer white wine or imported bottled water. They eat raw fish, but like their beef well done. Sushi, tofu, and French food are standard liberal fare.

Another interesting revolutionary side note: most of their women have higher testosterone levels than their men. Most social workers, doctors, attorneys, journalists, dreamers in Hollywood and group therapists are liberals. Liberals invented the designated hitter rule because it wasn't "fair" to make the pitcher also bat.

Conservatives drink domestic beer. They eat red meat and still provide for their women. Conservatives are big-game hunters, rodeo cowboys, lumberjacks, construction workers, firemen, police officers, Marines, athletes and generally anyone who works productively. Conservatives who own companies hire other conservatives.

Liberals produce little or nothing. They like to "govern" the producers and decide how to redistribute the production. Liberals believe Europeans are more enlightened than Americans. That is why most of the liberals remained in Europe when conservatives were coming to America. They crept in later, after the Wild West was tamed, and created a business of trying to get MORE for nothing.

Here ends today's lesson in world history and anthropology from the Conservative viewpoint.

Contributed by David Taylor

Cow One-Liners

10/11/2005

There are two cows standing in a field..
Cow 1: Moo!
Cow 2: Damn! I was gonna say that!

There are two cows standing in a field..
Cow 1: Say..you're not worried about this mad cow disease are you?
Cow 2: No..why should I be? I'm a helicopter!

There are two cows standing in a field..
A sheep walks up to them..
Sheep: Say lads, any chance of telling me which way to town?
Both cows stare blankly at the sheep..
Sheep: Do you speak English?
Both cows continue to stare blankly..
Sheep: Hello?! Oh,screw it!
The sheep walks off, and one cow turns to the other..
Cow: Wow! Did you see that? A talking sheep!

Contributed by Ron Gargasz

Cranky Old Man

10/15/2013

When an old man died in the geriatric ward of a nursing home in an Australian country town, it was believed that he had nothing left of any value. Later, when the nurses were going through his meager possessions, they found this poem.

Its quality and content so impressed the staff that copies were made and distributed to every nurse in the hospital.

One nurse took her copy to Melbourne. The old man's sole bequest to posterity has since appeared in the Christmas editions of magazines around the country and appearing in magazines for Mental Health. A slide presentation has also been made based on his simple, but eloquent, poem.

And this old man, with nothing left to give to the world, is now the author of this 'anonymous' poem winging across the Internet.

Cranky Old Man

What do you see nurses? … What do you see?
What are you thinking … when you're looking at me?
A cranky old man, … not very wise,
Uncertain of habit … with faraway eyes?
Who dribbles his food … and makes no reply.
When you say in a loud voice …'I do wish you'd try!'
Who seems not to notice … the things that you do.
And forever is losing … A sock or shoe?
Who, resisting or not … lets you do as you will,
With bathing and feeding … The long day to fill?
Is that what you're thinking? … Is that what you see?
Then open your eyes, nurse, you're not looking at me.
I'll tell you who I am … As I sit here so still,
As I do at your bidding, … as I eat at your will.
I'm a small child of Ten … with a father and mother,
Brothers and sisters … who love one another
A young boy of Sixteen … with wings on his feet
Dreaming that soon now … a lover he'll meet.
A groom soon at Twenty … my heart gives a leap.
Remembering, the vows … that I promised to keep.
At Twenty-Five, now … I have young of my own.
Who needs me to guide … And a secure happy home.
A man of Thirty … My young now grown fast,
Bound to each other … With ties that should last.
At Forty, my young sons … have grown and are gone,
But my woman is beside me … to see I don't mourn.
At Fifty, once more … Babies play 'round my knee,
Again, we know children … My loved one and me.
Dark days are upon me … My wife is now dead.
I look at the future … I shudder with dread.
For my young are all rearing … young of their own.
And I think of the years … And the love that I've known.
I'm now an old man … and nature is cruel.

It's jest to make old age ... look like a fool.
The body, it crumbles ... grace and vigor, depart.
There is now a stone ... where I once had a heart.
But inside this old carcass ... A young man still dwells,
And now and again ... my battered heart swells
I remember the joys ... I remember the pain.
And I'm loving and living ... life over again.
I think of the years, all too few ... gone too fast.
And accept the stark fact ... that nothing can last.
So, open your eyes, people ... open and see.
Not a cranky old man.
Look closer ... see ... ME!

Remember this poem when you next meet an older person who you might brush aside without looking at the young soul within. We will all, one day, be there, too!

Contributed by Barbara Wonderly

A Difficult Decision

11/8/2012

An old man was asked, «At your ripe age, what would you prefer to get - Parkinson›s or Alzheimer›s?»

The wise one answered, "Definitely Parkinson's. Better to spill half an ounce of Scotch than to forget where you kept the bottle!"

From Ron Gargasz

Don't Mess with Seniors

1/7/2011

A kid just out of college and a senior citizen were sitting next to each other on a long flight. The kid was of the opinion that seniors were so dumb that he could fool him easily. So, the kid asked if the senior would like to play a fun game.

The senior was tired and just wanted to take a nap, so he politely declined and tried to catch a few winks.

The kid persisted saying, "The game is a lot of fun. I ask you a question and if you don't know the answer, you pay me only $5. Then you ask me one, and if I don't know the answer, I will pay you $500."

This caught the senior's attention and, to keep the kid quiet, he agreed to play the game.

The kid asked the first question. "What's the distance from the Earth to the Moon?"

The senior didn't say a word but reached into his pocket, pulled out a five-dollar bill, and handed it to the kid. But now it was the senior's turn. He asked the kid, "What goes up a hill with three legs, and comes down with four?"

The kid used his laptop to search all the references he could find on the Internet and sent e-mails to all the smart friends he knew -- all to no avail.

After an hour of searching, he finally gave up. He woke the senior and handed him $500. The senior pocketed the $500 and went right back to sleep.

The kid was going nuts not knowing the answer. He woke the senior up and asks, "Well, so what does go up a hill with three legs and come down with four?"

The senior reached into his pocket, handed the kid $5 and went back to sleep.

Contributed by Ron Heisler

Drink Orders

7/19/2010

A French Mormon was seated next to an Irish Catholic on a flight from London. After the plane was airborne, drink orders were taken.

The Irishman asked for a whiskey, which was promptly brought and placed before him.

The flight attendant then asked the Mormon if he would like a drink.

He replied in disgust, "I'd rather be savagely raped by a dozen whores than let liquor touch my lips."

The Irishman then handed his drink back to the attendant and said, "Me too, I didn't know we had that choice."

Contributed by Judy Flahiff

Ear Hair

3/21/2024

Because my neighbor's dog could hardly hear, she took it to the veterinarian. He found that the problem was hair in its ears. After he cleaned both, the dog could hear fine.

The vet then proceeded to tell the owner that if she wanted to keep this from recurring, she should go to the store and get some "Nair" hair remover and rub it in the dog's ears once a month.

After leaving the vet, she stopped at the drug store and got some Nair. At the register, the druggist told her, "If you're going to use this under your arms, don't use deodorant for a few days."

She replied, "I'm not using it under my arms."

"Well, if you're using it on your legs, don't shave for a couple of days."

A bit miffed, she replied, "I'm not using it on my legs either. If you must know, I'm using it on my schnauzer."

The druggist then suggested, "Stay off your bicycle for a week."

Contributed by Gary Thornton

Eight False Things the Public "Knows"

10/30/2010

1) President Obama tripled the deficit.
Reality: Bush's last budget had a $1.416 trillion deficit. Obama's first budget reduced that to $1.29 trillion.

2) President Obama raised taxes, which hurt the economy.
Reality: Obama cut taxes. 40% of the "stimulus" was wasted on tax cuts which only create debt, which is why it was so much less effective than it could have been.

3) President Obama bailed out the banks.
Reality: While many people confuse the "stimulus" with the bank bailouts, the bank bailouts were requested by President Bush and his Treasury Secretary, former Goldman Sachs CEO Henry Paulson. (Paulson also wanted the bailouts to be "non-reviewable by any court or any agency.") The bailouts passed and began **before** the 2008 election of President Obama.

4) The stimulus didn't work.
Reality: The stimulus worked but was not enough. In fact, according to the Congressional Budget Office, the stimulus raised employment by between 1.4 million and 3.3 million jobs.

5) Businesses will hire if they get tax cuts.
Reality: A business hires the right number of employees to meet demand. Having extra cash does not cause a business to hire, but a business that

has a demand for what it does will find the money to hire. Businesses want customers, not tax cuts.

6) Health care reform costs $1 trillion.
Reality: The health care reform reduces government deficits by $138 billion.

7) Social Security is a Ponzi scheme, is "going broke," people live longer, fewer workers per retiree, etc.
Reality: Social Security has run a surplus since it began, has a trust fund in the trillions, is completely sound for at least 25 more years and cannot legally borrow so cannot contribute to the deficit (compare that to the military budget!) Life expectancy is only longer because fewer babies die; people who reach 65 live about the same number of years as they used to.

8) Government spending takes money out of the economy.
Reality: Government is "We, the People" and the money it spends is on "We, the People." Many people do not know that it is government that builds the roads, airports, ports, courts, schools and other things that are the soil in which business thrives. Many people think that all government spending is on "welfare" and "foreign aid" when that is only a small part of the government's budget.

Contributed by Donald O'Dell

Eight Morons from 2005

From 2/4/2006

1. WILL THE REAL DUMMY PLEASE STAND UP?

AT&T fired President John Walter after nine months, saying he lacked intellectual leadership. He received a $26 million severance package.

Perhaps it was not Walter who was lacking intelligence.

2. WITH A LITTLE HELP FROM OUR FRIENDS:

Police in Oakland, CA spent two hours attempting to subdue a gunman who had barricaded himself inside his home.

After firing ten tear gas canisters, officers discovered that the man was standing beside them in the police line shouting, "Please come out and give yourself up!"

3. WHAT WAS PLAN B?

An Illinois man, pretending to have a gun, kidnapped a motorist and forced him to drive to two different automated teller machines, wherein the kidnapper proceeded to withdraw money from his **own** bank accounts.

4. THE GETAWAY!

A man walked into a Topeka, KS Kwik Pick Stop and asked for all the money in the cash drawer.

Apparently the take was too small, so he tied up the store clerk and worked the counter himself for three hours until police showed up and grabbed him.

5. DID I SAY THAT???

Police in Los Angeles had good luck with a robbery suspect who just couldn't control himself during a lineup.

When detectives asked each man in the lineup to repeat the words: "Give me all your money or I'll shoot," the man shouted, "That's not what I said!"

6. ARE WE COMMUNICATING???

A man spoke frantically into the phone: «My wife is pregnant, and her contractions are only two minutes apart.»

"Is this her first child?" the doctor asked.

"No!" the man shouted, "This is her husband!"

7. NOT THE SHARPEST TOOL IN THE SHED!

In Modesto, CA, Steven Richard King was arrested for trying to hold up a Bank of America branch without a weapon. King used a thumb and a finger to simulate a gun.

Unfortunately, he failed to keep his hand in his pocket.

8. THE GRAND FINALE!

On Lake Isabella in the high desert an hour east of Bakersfield, CA, some folks new to boating were having a problem.

No matter how hard they tried, they couldn't get their brand new 22-foot boat going. It was very sluggish in almost every maneuver no matter how much power they applied.

After about an hour of trying to make it go, they putted into a nearby marina, thinking someone there may be able to tell them what was wrong.

A thorough topside check revealed everything in perfect working condition. The engine ran fine, the out-drive went up and down, and the propeller was the correct size and pitch.

So one of the marina guys jumped in the water to check underneath. He came up choking on water, he was laughing so hard.

NOW REMEMBER ..THIS IS TRUE.

Under the boat, still strapped securely in place .. was the trailer!

Contributed by David Taylor

Eight Tiny Reindeer
Threw Up in my Attic

12/12/2025

As septuagenarians who have lived in their home for some 38 years, the wife and I made the decision to downsize our collection of Christmas paraphernalia.

Literally one-half of our attic consisted of over a dozen twenty-seven-gallon storage tubs, eight large boxes, four black garbage bags, and a partridge in a pear tree.

"Honey," the wife said to me, "I just looked in the attic, and it looks like Santa, his elves, and eight tiny reindeer threw up in there. We have got to do some yuletide purging."

"I understand what you're saying. The last time I shut the attic door, one of the three wise men's legs was hanging out. I had to stuff it back up there under a camel's butt."

"This is not going to be easy," the wife instructed. "There are so many ornaments and decorations that we are sentimentally attached to, but we can't keep everything. It's just too much."

"Then how do we do this?" I asked afraid of her answer. "Because many of these ornaments I...."

"I know… (in a sing-song voice) you bought with your own money when you were ten years old. I hear that every Christmas. You can keep those. But ornaments that don't have a special meaning will have to go. Are you crying?"

"(Sniffing) No, I just got some dust in my eyes. Let's bring those bins down and get started."

So, I went up into the attic and started handing bin after bin, box after box, and bag after bag down to the wife in the garage.

"Is that all?" the wife asked.

"No, it's not. Balthasar's leg is still stuck in the camel's butt. I think I'm going to need forceps."

"Forget about Balthasar and the camel for now and let's start purging," the wife said.

And so, we started. And with every ornament came a story; the naughty clothespin angel smoking a cigarette that the son made at an advent workshop; the horrifying bangs on the daughter's third grade picture ornament; my one-legged Santa whose face I had to glue on last year; the wife's real wool Christmas sheep that loses its fur in the box every year.

It was very time consuming and very cathartic to examine each Christmas item and decide if it would be kept in our collection or neatly packaged to be donated to another family in need of Christmas decorations.

"Well," I said to the wife, "we are down to six bins and no boxes or bags. Do you think we did the right thing?"

"Yes, Honey, I think we did the right thing by blessing others with things we don't need any more."

"I guess you're right. But Balthasar's leg is still stuck in the camel's butt. What do we do about that?" I asked.

"I say we leave it there. It'll put a new twist on the nativity…"

Raul Ascunce

Estate Planning 101

7/12/2007

When Dan found out he was going to inherit a fortune when his sickly father died, he decided he needed a woman to enjoy it with -- so that evening he went to a singles bar where he spotted the most beautiful woman he had ever seen. Her natural beauty took his breath away.

"I may look like just an ordinary man," he said as he walked up to her, "but in just a week or two, my father will die and I'll inherit 20 million dollars."

Impressed, the woman went home with him that evening and, three days later, she became his stepmother.

(*Women are so much smarter than men.*)

Contributed by David Taylor

Fake Okies

September 22, 2005

Bubba Wayne and Billy Bob, who are both from Denton, Texas, traveled to Grand Lake, Oklahoma for a vacation. While walking along a busy downtown street, they saw a sign in a store window which read, "Suits $5.00 each, Shirts $2.00 each and Trousers $2.50 a pair."

Bubba Wayne said, "Woo Hoo, Billy Bob! We could buy a whole gob of these clothes, take 'em back to Denton, sell 'em to all our friends and make a fortune fer us."

He continued, "Now when we go in there, don't you say a word, okay? Just let me do the talkin' 'cause if they hear your Texas accent, they might think we're ignorant, and they won't wanna sell them clothes to us. Now, I'll talk in a slow, fake Oklahoma drawl so's they won't know."

They went in and Bubba Wayne said with his best Oklahoma drawl, "I'll take 50 of them thar suits at $5.00 each, 100 of them thar shirts at $2.00 each, and 50 pairs of them thar trousers at $2.50 each. I'll just back up my pickup and..."

The owner of the shop interrupted, "Ya'll from Texas, ain't ya?"

"Well..yeah," says a surprised Bubba Wayne. "How come'd you know that?"

The owner replied, "Cause up here we call this kind of store a 'dry cleaner!'"

Contributed by Ron Heisler

Fancy Supermarket

7/3/2006

The new Supermarket near our house has an automatic water mister to keep the produce fresh. Just before it goes on, you hear the sound of a thunderstorm and the smell of fresh rain.

When you approach the milk cases, you hear cows mooing and witness the scent of fresh butter fat.

When you approach the egg case, you hear hens cackle and the air is filled with the pleasing aroma of eggs frying.

So far, I have been too afraid to go down the toilet paper aisle.

Contributed by Ron Heisler

Flying Tips

9/5/2007

During a commercial airline flight, a Navy Pilot was seated next to a young mother with a babe in arms. When the baby began crying during the descent for landing, the mother began nursing the infant as discreetly as possible.

The pilot pretended not to notice, and, upon debarking, he gallantly offered his assistance to help with the various baby-related impedimenta. When the young mother expressed her gratitude, the pilot responded, "Gosh, that's a good-looking baby..and he sure was hungry!"

Somewhat embarrassed, the mother explained that her pediatrician said nursing would help alleviate the pressure in the baby's ears upon descent.

The Navy pilot sadly shook his head, and in true fighter pilot fashion exclaimed, "Damn! And all these years I've been chewing gum!"

Contributed by Bubba Mehling

For The Older Crowd

1/27/2011

A distraught senior citizen phoned her doctor's office. "Is it true," she wanted to know, "that the medication you prescribed has to be taken for the rest of my life?"

"Yes, I'm afraid so," the doctor told her.

There was a moment of silence before the senior lady replied, "I'm wondering, then, just how serious is my condition because this prescription is marked "NO REFILLS!"

An older gentleman was on the operating table awaiting surgery and he insisted that his son, a renowned surgeon, perform the operation. As he was about to get the anesthesia, he asked to speak to his son.

"Yes, Dad, what is it?"

"Don't be nervous, son! Do your best and just remember, if it doesn't go well, if something happens to me, your mother is going to come and live with you and your wife."

Eventually you will reach a point when you stop lying about your age and start bragging about it. This is so true. I love to hear them say "you don't look that old."

The older we get; the fewer things seem worth waiting in line for.

Some people try to turn back their odometers. Not me! I want people to know why I look this way. I've traveled a long way and some of the roads weren't paved.

When you are dissatisfied and would like to go back to youth, think of Algebra.

You know you are getting old when everything either dries up or leaks.

One of the many things no one tells you about aging is that it is such a nice change from being young. Being young is beautiful, but being old is comfortable.

First you forget names, then you forget faces. Then you forget to pull up your zipper ... but it's worse when you forget to pull it down.

Two guys .. one old, one young ... are pushing their carts around Wal-Mart when they collide. The older guy says to the younger guy, "Sorry about that. I'm looking for my wife, and I guess I wasn't paying attention to where I was going."

The young guy says, "That's OK, it's a coincidence. I'm looking for my wife, too. I can't find her and I'm getting a little desperate."

The old guy says, "Well, maybe I can help you find her. What does she look like?"

"Well, she is 27 years old, tall, with red hair, blue eyes, is buxom wearing no bra, long legs, and is wearing short shorts. What does your wife look like?"

To which the old guy says, "Doesn't matter, --- let's look for yours."

Contributed by Dawn Heisler

Getting Heavier

8/11/2005

"We all get heavier as we get older because
there's a lot more information in our heads."

So I'm not fat; I'm just really intelligent and my head couldn't
hold any more so it started filling up the rest of me!

That's my story and I'm sticking to it.

Contributed by David Taylor

God & The Blonde

10/11/2007

A blonde found herself in serious trouble. Her business had gone bust and she was in dire financial straits. She was so desperate that she decided to ask God for help. She began to pray, "God, please help me. I've lost my business and if I don't get some money, I'm going to lose my house as well. Please let me win the Lottery."

Lottery night came and somebody else won. She again prayed, "God, please let me win the Lottery! I've lost my business, my house, and now I'm going to lose my car as well."

Lottery night came again and she still had no luck. Once again, she prayed, "My God, why have you forsaken me? I've lost my business, my house, and my car. My children are starving. I don't often ask you for help and I have always been a good servant to you. Please let me win the Lottery just this one time so I can get my life back in order."

Suddenly there was a blinding flash of light as the heavens opened. The blonde was overwhelmed by the voice of God himself ... "Sweetheart, Work with Me on This ... Buy A Ticket!!!"

Contributed by Jim Greenwood

Golf Explained

11/17/2010

Golf can best be defined as an endless series of tragedies obscured
by the occasional miracle, followed by a good bottle of beer.

* * * * *

Golf! You hit down to make the ball go up. You swing
left and the ball goes right. The lowest score wins. And
on top of that, the winner buys the drinks.

* * * * *

Golf is harder than baseball. In golf, you have to play your foul balls.

* * * * *

If you find you do not mind playing golf in the rain, the snow, even
during a hurricane, here's a valuable tip: your life is in trouble.

* * * * *

Golfers who try to make everything perfect before
taking the shot rarely make a perfect shot.

* * * * *

The term "mulligan" is really a contraction of the phrase "maul it again."

* * * * *

A "gimme" can best be defined as an agreement between
two golfers .. neither of whom can putt very well.

* * * * *

An interesting thing about golf is that no matter how
badly you play; it's always possible to get worse.

* * * * *

Golf's a hard game to figure. One day you'll go out and slice
it and shank it, hit into all the traps and miss every green. The
next day you go out and for no reason at all you really stink.

* * * * *

If your best shots are the practice swing and the "gimme
putt," you might wish to reconsider this game.

* * * * *

Golf is the only sport where the most feared opponent is you.

* * * * *

Golf is like marriage: If you take yourself too seriously
it won't work, and both are expensive.

* * * * *

The best wood in most amateurs' bags is the pencil.

Contributed by Ron Heisler

Halloween Definitions

10/31/2007

Boogieman: The guy who passes time at a stoplight picking his nose.

Coffin: What you do when you get a piece of popcorn stuck in your throat.

Frankenstein: Hot dog and a mug of beer.

Full Moon: What your repairman reveals when he bends over to fix your fridge.

Goblin: How you eat the Snickers bars you got for Halloween.

Invisible Man: What a guy becomes when there's housework to be done.

Jack O' Lantern: An Irish Pumpkin.

Jack the Ripper: What Jack does to his lottery tickets after losing each week.

Mummy: The person who kisses the boo-boo after you scrape your knee.

Pumpkin Patch: What a pumpkin wears when trying to quit smoking.

Skeleton: Any supermodel.

Vampire Bat: What Dracula hits a baseball with.

Zombie: What you look like before that first cup of morning coffee.

Contributed by Tom Benner

Hey! Wasn't This Us?

10/21/2010

A little house with three bedrooms,
one bathroom and one car on the street.
A mower that you had to push
to make the grass look neat.

In the kitchen on the wall
we only had one phone,
And no need for recording things,
someone was always home.

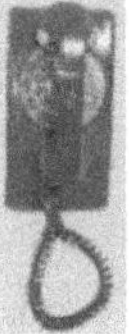

We only had a living room
where we would congregate,
unless it was at mealtime
in the kitchen where we ate.

We had no need for family rooms
or extra rooms to dine.
When meeting as a family
those two rooms would work out fine.

We only had one TV set
and channels maybe two,
But always there was one of them
with something worth the view.

For snacks we had potato chips
that tasted like a chip.
And if you wanted flavor
there was Lipton's onion dip.

Store-bought snacks were rare because
my mother liked to cook
and nothing can compare to snacks
in Betty Crocker's book.

Weekends were for family trips
or staying home to play.
We all did things together --
even go to church to pray.

When we did our weekend trips
depending on the weather,
no one stayed at home because
we liked to be together.

Sometimes we would separate
to do things on our own,
but we knew where the others were
without our own cell phone.

Then there were the movies
with your favorite movie star,
and nothing can compare
to watching movies in your car.

**Then there were the picnics
at the peak of summer season,
pack a lunch and find some trees
and never need a reason.**

**Get a baseball game together
with all the friends you know,
have real action playing ball --
and no game video.**

**Remember when the doctor
used to be the family friend,
and didn't need insurance
or a lawyer to defend?**

The way that he took care of you
or what he had to do,
because he took an oath and strived
to do the best for you.

Remember going to the store
and shopping casually,
and when you went to pay for it
you used your own money?

Nothing that you had to swipe
or punch in some amount,
and remember when the cashier person
had to really count?

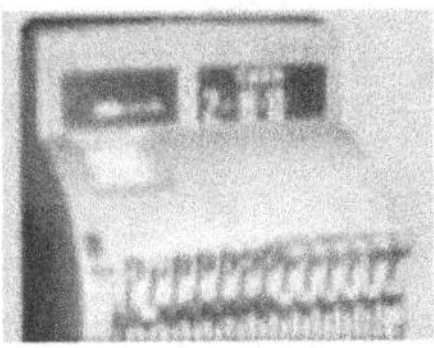

The milkman used to go
from door to door,
And it was just a few cents more
than going to the store.

There was a time when mailed letters
came right to your door,
without a lot of junk mail ads
sent out by every store.

The mailman knew each house by name
and knew where it was sent;
there were not loads of mail addressed
to "present occupant."

There was a time when just one glance
was all that it would take,
and you would know the kind of car,
the model and the make.

They didn't look like turtles
trying to squeeze out every mile;
they were streamlined, white walls, fins
and really had some style.

One time the music that you played
whenever you would jive,
was from a vinyl, big-holed record
called a forty-five.

The record player had a post
to keep them all in line
and then the records would drop down
and play one at a time.

Oh sure, we had our problems then,
just like we do today
and always we were striving,
trying for a better way.

Oh, the simple life we lived
still seems like so much fun,
how can you explain a game,
just kick the can and run?

W.G. Williams

**And why would boys put baseball cards
between bicycle spokes
and for a nickel, red machines
had little bottled Cokes?**

**This life seemed so much easier
and slower in some ways.
I love the new technology
but I sure do miss those days.**

**So time moves on and so do we
and nothing stays the same,
but I sure love to reminisce
and walk down memory lane.**

Contributed by Ron Heisler

How To Give a Cat a Pill

5/7/2010

1. Pick up cat and cradle it in the crook of your left arm as if holding a baby.

Position right forefinger and thumb on either side of cat's mouth and gently apply pressure to cheeks while holding pill in right hand. As cat opens mouth, pop pill into mouth.

Allow cat to close mouth and swallow.

2. Retrieve pill from floor and cat from behind sofa.

Cradle cat in left arm and repeat process.

3. Retrieve cat from bedroom and throw soggy pill away.

Take new pill from foil wrap, cradle cat in left arm, holding rear paws tightly with left hand.

Force jaws open and push pill to back of mouth with right forefinger. Hold mouth shut for a count of ten.

4. Retrieve pill from goldfish bowl and cat from top of wardrobe.

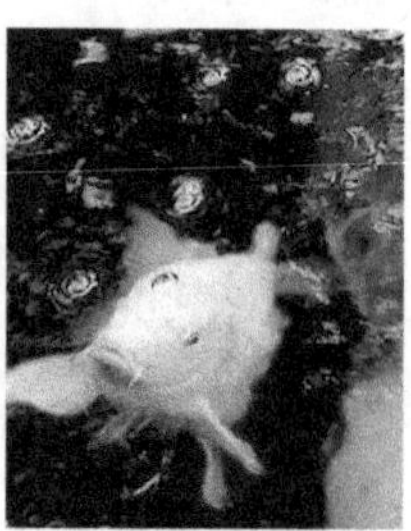

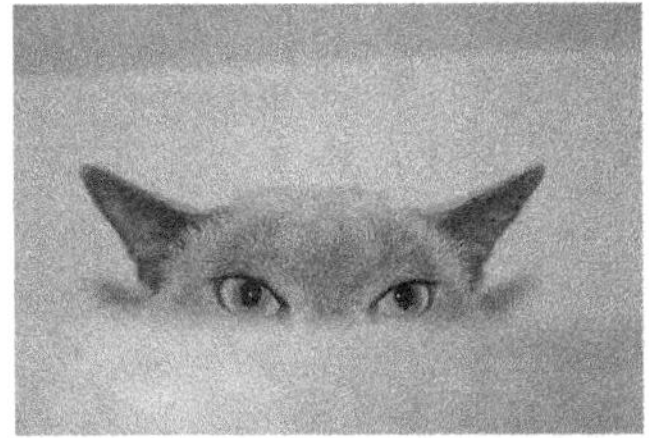

Call spouse in from the garden.

5. Kneel on floor with cat wedged firmly between knees, hold front and rear paws.

Ignore low growls emitted by cat. Get spouse to hold head firmly with one hand while forcing wooden ruler into mouth. Drop pill down ruler and rub cat's throat vigorously.

6. Retrieve cat from curtain rail.

Get another pill from foil wrap. Make note to buy new ruler and repair curtains. Carefully sweep shattered figurines and vases from hearth and set to one side for gluing later.

7. Wrap cat in large towel and get spouse to lie on cat with head just visible from below armpit.

Put pill in end of drinking straw, force mouth open with pencil and blow down drinking straw.

8. Check label to make sure pill not harmful to humans and drink one beer to take taste away.

Apply band-aid to spouse's forearm and remove blood from carpet with cold water and soap.

9. Retrieve cat from neighbor's shed.

Get another pill. Open another beer. Place cat in cupboard, and close door onto neck, to leave head showing. Force mouth open with dessert spoon. Flick pill down throat with elastic band.

10. Fetch screwdriver from garage and put cupboard door back on hinges. Drink beer. Fetch bottle of scotch. Pour shot, drink.

Apply cold compress to cheek and check records for date of last tetanus shot. Apply whiskey compress to cheek to disinfect. Toss back another shot. Throw tee-shirt away and fetch new one from bedroom.

11. Call fire department to retrieve the damn cat from the top of the tree across the road. Apologize to neighbor who crashed into fence while swerving to avoid cat.

Take last pill from foil wrap.

12. Using heavy-duty pruning gloves from shed, tie the little *&#%^'s front paws to rear paws with garden twine and bind tightly to leg of dining table. Push pill into mouth followed by large piece of filet steak.

Be rough about it. Hold head vertically and pour two pints of water down throat to wash pill down.

13. Consume remainder of scotch.

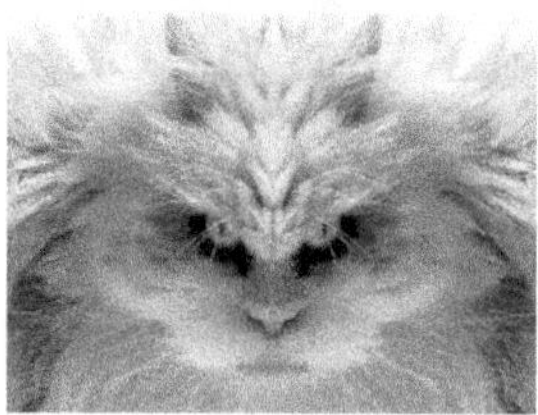

Get spouse to drive you to the emergency room. Sit quietly while doctor stitches fingers and forearm and removes pill remnants from right eye. Call furniture shop on way home to order new table.

14. Arrange for RSPCA to collect mutant cat from hell and call local pet shop to see if they have any hamsters.

How To Give A Dog A Pill

1. Wrap it in bacon.
2. Toss it in the air.

Contributed by E.W. Hallford

How To Tell If You Need to Pray at Work

October 7, 2005

When a co-worker comes in a little too happy singing "good morning" to everyone and you think, "Somebody needs to slap the s#@! out of her"... You need to pray at work.

When someone comes in and announces, "office meeting in 5 minutes," and you think, "what the f*&% do they want now?"... You need to pray at work.

When your computer is mysteriously turned off and you want to say, "which one of you sons of b*&^%$# turned off my computer?"... You need to pray at work.

When you and a co-worker are discussing something and a third person comes in and says, "well at my last office ..." and you want to throw a stapler at him ... You need to pray at work.

When you hear a co-worker call your name and the first thing that crosses your mind is, "what the h*&^ does she want now?" and you try to hide underneath your desk .... You need to pray at work.

When you are asked to stay late and help do someone else's work and the first thing that pops into your head is, "both of y'all can kiss my a@@!!"... You need to pray at work.

When you're in the elevator and it stops to pick up someone who stood for five minutes waiting for the darn thing only to go DOWN one floor, and you say "that lazy b*&%$#"... You need to pray at work.

When you take some vacation time and come back to find a mountain of paperwork sitting on your desk because no one else would do it and you think, "sorry a## M#$^%F%&#s".... You need to pray at work.

If you have ever thought about poisoning, choking, punching, slapping or flattening someone's tires that you work with ... You need to pray at work.

If you avoid saying more than hello or how are you doing to someone because you know it's going to lead to their life story .... You need to pray at work.

If you know all the words that have been bleeped out, you need to pray at work!

LET US ALL BOW OUR HEADS

Contributed by John Hunt

I Gotta Go

8/17/2010

72-year-old Emma laughs at aging and tells this story on herself:

"One day a policeman pulled me over for speeding. I was guilty but I didn't want a ticket. Who would?

"As the officer approached, I started moving rapidly from side to side. He noticed and asked if I was all right. I said that I had to use the toilet and a woman my age can't hold it very easily.

"I didn't have to use the toilet, but I needed an excuse to get out of that speeding ticket. The officer believed me and told me to drive the speed limit to the nearest bathroom.

"As I drove off, I laughed at my prank. The more I thought about it, the harder I laughed. Soon I was laughing so hard that I really did have to pee. That made me laugh even more. Finally, I was laughing so hard that I went.

"I pulled over ... not because I wet myself but because my teeth had fallen into my lap!"

WG. Williams

If You Marry a Texas Girl

2/4/2020

Three friends married women from different parts of the country. The first man married a woman from Utah. He told her that she was to do the dishes and house cleaning. It took a couple of days, but on the third day, he came home to see a clean house and dishes washed and put away.

The second man married a woman from North Carolina. He gave his wife orders that she was to do all the cleaning, dishes, and the cooking. The first day he didn't see any results, but the next day he saw it was better. By the third day, he saw his house was clean, the dishes were done, and there was a huge dinner on the table.

The third man married a girl from Texas. He ordered her to keep the house cleaned, dishes washed, lawn mowed, laundry washed, and hot meals on the table for every meal. He said that the first day he didn't see anything, the second day he didn't see anything but by the third day some of the swelling had gone down and he could see a little out of his left eye, and his arm was healed enough that he could fix himself a sandwich and load the dishwasher.

He still has some difficulty when he pees.

Wells Teague

It's In the Verbiage

8/6/2007

A Catholic priest and a Protestant minister are standing along the road pounding a sign into the ground that reads:

The End is Near!
Turn Yourself Around Now,
Before it's Too Late!

As a car speeds past them, the driver yells, "Leave us alone, you religious nuts!" Around the curve ahead they heard screeching tires and a big splash.

The priest turns to the minister and says, "Maybe the sign should just say 'Bridge Out.'"

Contributed by Ron Gargasz

Just Like a Man

(Through HIS Eyes)
8/15/2024

A wife was curious when she found two old negatives in a drawer and had them made into prints.

She was pleasantly surprised to see that they were of her at a much younger, slimmer time, taken many years ago on one of her first dates with her husband.

When she showed him the photos, his face lit up. "Wow, look at that!," he said with appreciation,

"That's my old Ford!"

Contributed by Ron Gargasz

Life With the Circus

1/3/2024

A couple who worked in a circus went to an adoption agency. There the social workers questioned their suitability.

The couple produced photos of their 50-foot motor home which was equipped with a beautiful nursery.

Even with that the social workers were doubtful about the education that the child would get."

We've arranged for a full-time tutor who will teach the child all the usual subjects along with French, Mandarin, and even computer skills."

But there were still doubts about raising a child in the circus environment.

They explained that "Our nanny is an expert in pediatric welfare and diet."

Finally, the social workers were satisfied and asked, "What age child are you hoping to adopt?"

"It doesn't really matter as long as he fits in the cannon."

Contributed by Ron Gargasz

Little Known Illnesses

11/5/2007

AFROPHOBIA: Fear of the return of the 70's hair styles.

DEJA FLU: The feeling that one has had this cold before.

HYPOCOINDRIA: Fear of not having correct change.

HAIRPIECE SWIMPLEX: Rash caused by wearing a toupee in a pool.

HERPES CINEPLEX: Rash caused by movie tickets priced at $9.50.

CELESTIAL SEASONINGS AFFECTIVE DISORDER: Herbal-tea addiction.

VISACARDITIS: The heart-stopping sensation brought on by exceeding your credit limit.

SONSTROKE: An attack during the reading of a will.

ROSWELL-BABY SYNDROME: Irrational fear that one's infant might be an alien.

OREOPOROSIS: Disorder caused by too many cookies, not enough milk.

Contributed by Tom Benner

"M"

3/26/2008

Miss Jones had been giving her second-grade students a lesson on science. She had explained about magnets and showed how they would pick up nails and other bits of iron. Now it was question time and she asked, "My name begins with the letter 'M' and I pick up things. What am I?"

A little boy on the front row said, "You're a mother."

Contributed by Tom Benner

Math Symbols

7/31/2008

While reviewing math symbols with my second-grade pupils, I drew a greater-than (>) and a less-than sign (<) on the chalkboard and asked, "Does anyone remember what these mean?"

A few moments passed, and then a boy confidently raised his hand. "One means fast-forward," he exclaimed, "and the other means rewind!"

Contributed by Tom Benner

Medical Insurance Explained

7/31/2006

Q. What does HMO stand for?

This is actually a variation of the phrase, "HEY MOE." Its roots go back to a concept pioneered by Moe of the Three Stooges, who discovered that a patient could be made to forget the pain in his foot if he was poked hard enough in the eye.

Q. I just joined an HMO. How difficult will it be to choose the doctor I want?

Just slightly more difficult than choosing your parents. Your insurer will provide you with a book listing all the doctors in the plan. Doctors basically fall into two categories--those who are no longer accepting new patients, and those who will see you but are no longer participating in the plan. But don't worry, the remaining doctor who is still in the plan and accepting new patients has an office just a half-day's drive away and a diploma from a third world country.

Q. Do all diagnostic procedures require pre-certification?

No. Only those you need.

Q. Can I get coverage for my preexisting conditions?

Certainly, as long as they don't require any treatment.

Q. What happens if I want to try alternative forms of medicine?

You'll need to find alternative forms of payment.

Q. My pharmacy plan only covers generic drugs, but I need the name brand. I tried the generic medication, but it gave me a stomachache. What should I do?

Poke yourself in the eye.

Q. What if I'm away from home and I get sick?

You really shouldn't do that.

Q. I think I need to see a specialist, but my doctor insists he can handle my problem. Can a general practitioner really perform a heart transplant right in his/her office?

Hard to say but considering that all your risking is the $20 co-payment, there's no harm in giving it a shot.

Q. Will health care be different in the next century?

No, but if you call right now, you might get an appointment by then.

~ 101 ~

Contributed by David Taylor

Medicare Part G
The Nursing Home Plan

9/21/2023

A zero premium, no deductible Long Term Health Care Plan

Say you are an older senior citizen and can no longer
take care of yourself and need Long-Term Care
… but the government says there's no Nursing
Home care available for you.
So, what do you do?
You opt for Medicare Part G.

The plan gives anyone 75 or older a gun (Part G) and one bullet.
You're allowed to shoot one worthless politician.
This means you will be sent to prison for the rest of your life where you
will receive three meals a day, a roof over your head, central heating and
air conditioning, cable TV, a library, and all the health care you need.

Need new teeth? No problem. Need glasses? That's great.
Need a hearing aid, new hip, knees, kidney, lungs,
sex change, or heart? They're all covered!

As an added bonus, your kids can come and visit
you at least as often as they do now!

And who will be paying for all of this?

The same government that just told you they can't
afford for you to go into a nursing home.
And you will get rid of a useless politician while you are at it.
And now, because you are a prisoner, you don't
have to pay any more income taxes!

Is this a great country or what?

Now that you have solved your senior Long-Term
Care problem, enjoy the rest of your week!

Contributed by Susan Luna

Memo To My Pets

1/17/2006

The dishes with the paw print are yours and contain your food. The other dishes are mine and contain my food. Please note, placing a paw print in the middle of my plate and food does not stake a claim for it becoming your food and dish, nor do I find that aesthetically pleasing in the slightest.

* The stairway was not designed by NASCAR and is not a race-track. Beating me to the bottom is not the object. Tripping me doesn't help because I fall faster than you can run.
* I cannot buy anything bigger than a king-sized bed. I am very sorry about this. Do not think I will continue sleeping on the couch to ensure your comfort. Dogs and cats can actually curl up in a ball when they sleep. It is not necessary to sleep perpendicular to each other stretched out to the fullest extent possible. I also know that sticking tails straight out and having tongues hanging out the other end to maximize space is nothing but sarcasm.
* For the last time, there is not a secret exit from the bathroom. If by some miracle I beat you there and manage to get the door shut, it is not necessary to claw, whine, meow, try to turn the knob or get your paw under the edge and try to pull the door open. I must exit through the same door I entered. Also, I have been using the bathroom for years-canine or feline attendance is not mandatory.
* The proper order is kiss me, then go smell the other dog or cat's butt. I cannot stress this enough!

To pacify you, my dear pets, I have posted the following message on our front door:

Rules for Non-Pet Owners Who Visit and Like to Complain About Our Pets:

1. **They live here. You don't.**
2. **If you don't want their hair on your clothes, stay off the furniture. (That's why they call it "fur"niture.)**
3. **I like my pets a lot better than most people.**
4. **To you, it's an animal. To me, he/she is an adopted son/daughter who is short, hairy, walks on all fours and doesn't speak clearly.**

Dogs and cats are better than kids. They eat less, don't ask for money all the time, are easier to train, usually come when called, never drive your car, don't hang out with drug-using friends, don't smoke or drink, don't worry about having to buy the latest fashions, don't wear your clothes, and don't need a gazillion dollars for college - and if they get pregnant, you can sell the children.

Contributed by David Taylor

Memorial Day 2006

5/26/2006

*Just a little something I would like to pass on
to all of you .. something I would like you to join
me in doing on May 29, 2006, Memorial Day.*

*At 3 p.m. on Memorial Day, Major League Baseball
games will stop, Amtrak train whistles will blast,
and thousands of Americans will pause for the
Memorial Day National Moment of Remembrance.*

*Nascar, military installations, veterans service
organizations, schools, universities, hospitals,
national parks, airports, bus lines, and the
International Space Station will also join in.*

*What I am asking you is, wherever you are
or whatever you are doing at 3 p.m, PLEASE
join in this nationwide moment of reflection.*

A great man once said:
"And so, my fellow Americans, ask not what
your country can do for you;
ask what you can do for your country."

It's time for us to stand together and show
our support for our Military now and for
those who died fighting for the freedoms
we all enjoy today. It's time to be
an American!
My Thanks to all of you.

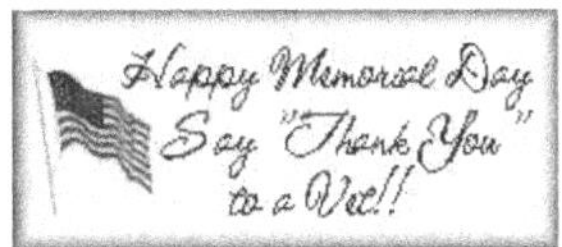

W.G. Williams

My Wish for You in 2007

12/31/2006

* May peace break into your house and may thieves come to steal your debts.
* May the pockets of your jeans become a magnet for $100 bills.
* May love stick to your face like Vaseline and may laughter assault your lips!
* May your clothes smell of success like smoking tires, may happiness slap you across the face, and may your tears be that of joy.
* May the problems you had forget your home address!
*
* In simple words .. **May 2007 be the best year of your life!!!**

Contributed by Bubba & Bonnie Mehling

Never Tick Off a Nurse

6/28/2006

A big shot attorney had to spend a couple of days in the hospital. He was a royal pain to the nurses because he bossed them around just like he did his staff. None of the hospital staff wanted to have anything to do with him.

The head nurse was the only one who could stand up to him, but finally even she had had enough. She came into his room and announced, "I have to take your temperature."

After complaining for several minutes, he finally settled down, crossed his arms and opened his mouth. "No, I'm sorry," the nurse stated, "but for this reading, I can't use an oral thermometer." This started another round of complaining, but eventually he rolled over and bared his behind.

After feeling the nurse insert the thermometer, he heard her announce, "I have to get something. Now you stay JUST LIKE THAT until I get back!"

She left the door to his room open on her way out. He cursed under his breath as he heard people walking past his door, laughing. After a half hour, the man's doctor came into the room. "What's going on here?" he asked.

Angrily, the man answered, "What's the matter, Doc? Haven't you ever seen someone having their temperature taken?"

After a pause, the doctor confessed, "Not with a carnation."

Contributed by Ron Gargasz

New Element Found!!!

12/7/2005

The recent hurricanes and skyrocketing oil and gasoline prices helped to prove the existence of a new element. In early October 2005, a major research institution announced the discovery of the heaviest element yet known to science. The new element has been named "Governmentium."

Governmentium (Gv) has one neutron, 25 assistant neutrons, 88 deputy neutrons, and 198 assistant deputy neutrons, giving it an atomic mass of 312. These 312 particles are held together by forces called 'morons' which are surrounded by vast quantities of lepton-like particles called 'peons.' Since Gv has no electrons, it is inert. However, it can be detected, because it impedes every reaction with which it comes into contact. A minute amount of Gv causes one reaction to take over four days to complete, when it would normally take less than a second!

Gv has a normal half-life of 4 years; it does not decay; but instead undergoes a reorganization in which a portion of the assistant neutrons and deputy neutrons exchange places. In fact, Governmentium's mass will actually increase over time, since each reorganization will cause more morons to become neutrons, forming 'isodopes.' This characteristic of moron promotion leads most scientists to believe that Gv is formed whenever morons reach a certain quantity in concentration. This hypothetical quantity is referred to as 'Critical Morass.'

When catalyzed with money, Gv becomes "Administratium' (Am) - an element which radiates just as much energy as Gv, since it has half as many peons but twice as many morons.

Contributed by Fred Schroeder

New Orleans Crabs

11/21/2008

A man boarded an airplane in New Orleans with a box of frozen crabs and asked a blonde, female crew member to take care of the box for him. She took the box and promised to put it in the crew's refrigerator.

He pointedly advised her that he was holding her personally responsible for the crabs staying frozen, mentioned that he was a lawyer, and proceeded to rant at her about what would happen if she let them thaw out.

Needless to say, she was annoyed by his behavior.

Shortly before landing in New York, she used the intercom to announce to the entire cabin, "Would the gentleman who gave me the crabs in New Orleans, please raise your hand?"

Not one hand went up .. so she took them home and ate them herself.

Two lessons here:

1. Men never learn.
2. Blondes aren't as dumb as most men think.

Contributed by Linda Anderson

A New Wine for Seniors

7/13/2005

A new wine for seniors

California vintners in the Napa Valley area, which primarily produces Pinot Blanc, Pinot Noir and Pinot Grigio wines, have developed a new hybrid grape that acts as an anti-diuretic. It is expected to reduce the number of trips older people have to make to the bathroom during the night.

The new wine will be marketed as Pino More.

Contributed by Julius Graw

News Bulletin

12/6/2005

This morning -- from a cave somewhere in Pakistan -- Taliban Minister of Migration, Mohammed Omar warned the United States that if military action against Iraq continues, Taliban authorities will cut off America's supply of convenience store managers. If this action does not yield sufficient results, cab drivers will be next.

It's getting ugly.

Contributed by David Taylor

The No-Excuse Sunday

10/13/2005

In order to make it possible for everyone to attend church this weekend, your local congregation is planning a special no-excuse Sunday.

1. Cots will be placed in the vestibule for those who say, "Sunday is my only day for sleeping in."
2. Eye drops will be available for those whose eyes are tired from watching TV too late on Saturday night.
3. We will have steel helmets for those who believe the roof will cave in if they show up for church.
4. Blankets will be provided for those who complain that the church is too cold. Fans will be on hand for those who say the church is too hot.
5. We will have hearing aids for the parishioners who say, "The pastor talks too loud."
6. Score cards will be available for those who wish to count the hypocrites.
7. We guarantee that some relatives will be present for those who like to go visiting on Sunday.
8. There will be TV dinners available for those who claim they can't go to church and cook dinner too.
9. One section of the church will have some trees and grass for those who see God in nature, especially on the golf course.

10. The sanctuary will be decorated with both Christmas poinsettias and Easter lilies to create a familiar environment for those who have never seen the church without them.

Contributed by Bonnie & Bubba Mehling

A Note for Artists

10/12/2023

Contributed by David A. Silverman

Nuns Are People Too

2/1/2024

Sisters Mary Catherine, Maria Theresa, Katherine Marie, Rose Frances, & Mary Kathleen left their convent on a trip to St. Patrick's Cathedral in New York City and were sight-seeing on a Tuesday in July.

It was hot and humid in town and their traditional garb was making them so uncomfortable that they decided to stop in at Paddy McGuire's Pub for a cold soft drink.

Paddy had recently added special legs to his barstools, which were the talk of the fashionable eastside neighborhood. All five nuns sat up at the bar and were enjoying their Cokes when Monsignor Riley and Father McGinty entered the bar through the front door.

They, too, came for a cold drink when they were shocked and almost fainted at what they saw.

Give us a sense of humor, Lord,
Give us the grace to see a joke,
To get some humor out of life,
And pass it on to other folk.

Contributed by Linda Narges

Obama's Use of Complete Sentences Stirs Controversy

Stunning Break with Last Eight Years
11/24/2008

In the first two weeks since the election, President-elect Barack Obama has broken with a tradition established over the past eight years through his controversial use of complete sentences, political observers say.

Millions of Americans who watched Mr. Obama's appearance on CBS' "Sixty Minutes" on Sunday witnessed the president-elect's unorthodox verbal tic, which had Mr. Obama employing grammatically correct sentences virtually every time he opened his mouth.

But Mr. Obama's decision to use complete sentences in his public pronouncements carries with it certain risks since, after the last eight years, many Americans may find his odd speaking style jarring.

According to presidential historian Davis Logsdon of Tulane University, some Americans might find it "alienating" to have a President who speaks English as if it were his first language.

"Every time Obama opens his mouth, his subjects and verbs are in agreement," says Mr. Logsdon. "If he keeps it up, he is running the risk of sounding like an elitist."

The historian said that if Mr. Obama insists on using complete sentences in his speeches, the public may find itself saying, "Okay, subject, predicate, subject predicate - we get it, stop showing off."

The President-elect's stubborn insistence on using complete sentences has already attracted a rebuke from one of his harshest critics, Gov. Sarah Palin of Alaska.

"Talking with complete sentences there and also too talking in a way that ordinary Americans like Joe the Plumber and Tito the Builder can't really do there, I think needing to do that isn't tapping into what Americans are needing also," she said.

~ 119 ~

Contributed by Bill D'Antonio

Old Goats

8/22/2006

A group of Canadians was traveling by tour bus through Holland. As they stopped at a cheese farm, a young guide led them through a process of cheese making, explaining that goat's milk was used.

She showed the group a lively hillside where many goats were grazing. These, she explained, were the older goats put out to pasture when they no longer produced.

She then asked, "What do you do in Canada with your old goats that aren't producing?"

A spry old gentleman answered. "They send us on bus tours."

Contributed by Bubba & Bonnie Mehling

Old Hillbilly Wisdom:

11/24/2022

Your fences need to be horse-high, pig-tight and bull-strong.

Keep skunks, bankers, and politicians at a distance.

Life is simpler when you plow around the stump.

A bumble bee is considerably faster than a John Deere tractor.

Words that soak into your ears are whispered, not yelled.

The best sermons are lived, not preached.

If you don't take the time to do it right,
you'll find the time to do it twice.

Don't corner something that is meaner than you.

Don't pick a fight with an old man. If he is
too old to fight, he'll just kill you.

It don't take a very big person to carry a grudge.

You cannot unsay a cruel word.

Every path has a few puddles.

When you wallow with pigs, expect to get dirty.

Don't be banging your shin on a stool that's not in the way.

Borrowing trouble from the future doesn't deplete the supply.

Most of the stuff people worry about ain't never gonna happen anyway.

Don't judge folks by their relatives.

Silence is sometimes the best answer.

Don't interfere with somethin' that ain't botherin' you none.

Timing has a lot to do with the outcome of a rain dance.

If you find yourself in a hole, the first thing to do is stop diggin'.

Sometimes you get, and sometimes you get got.

The biggest troublemaker you'll ever have to deal with
watches you from the mirror every mornin'.

Always drink upstream from the herd.

Good judgment comes from experience, and
most of that comes from bad judgment.

Lettin' the cat outta the bag is a whole lot easier than puttin' it back in.

If you get to thinkin' you're a person of some influence,
try orderin' somebody else's dog around.

Live a good, honorable life. Then when you get older
and think back, you'll enjoy it a second time.

Live simply. Love generously. Care deeply.
Speak kindly. Leave the rest to God.

Most times, it just gets down to common sense.

W.G. Williams

On Football Players

11/11/2012

Ohio State's Urban Meyer on one of his players:
"He doesn't know the meaning of the word fear. In fact, I just saw his grades and he doesn't know the meaning of a lot of words."

Why do Tennessee fans wear orange?
So they can dress that way for the game on Saturday, go hunting on Sunday, and pick up trash on Monday.

What does the average Alabama player get on his SATs?
Drool.

How many University of South Carolina freshmen football players does it take to change a light bulb?
None. That's a sophomore course.

How did the Georgia football player die from drinking milk?
The cow fell on him.

Two West Virginia football players were walking in the woods. One of them said, "Look, a dead bird."
The other looked up in the sky and said, "Where?"

A University of Cincinnati football player was almost killed yesterday in a tragic horseback-riding accident.
He fell from a horse and was nearly trampled to death.
Luckily, the manager of the Wal-Mart came out and unplugged the horse.

What do you say to a University of South Carolina football player dressed in a three-piece suit?
"Will the defendant please rise."

If three Florida State football players are in the same car, who is driving?
The police officer.

How can you tell if an Auburn football player has a girlfriend?
There's tobacco juice on both sides of the pickup truck.

What do you get when you put 32 Arkansas cheerleaders in one room?
A full set of teeth.

University of Michigan Coach Brady Hoke is only going to dress half of his players for the game this week; .. the other half will have to dress themselves.

How is the Indiana football team like an opossum?
They play dead at home and get killed on the road.

Why did the Nebraska linebacker steal a police car?
He saw "911" on the side and thought it was a Porsche.

How do you get a former Illinois football player off your porch?
Pay him for the pizza.

What are the longest three years of a University of Alabama football player's life?
Freshman I, Freshman II, and Freshman III.

From Julius Graw

Passwords

4/9/2010

During a company's recent password audit, it was found that a blonde employee was using the following password:

"MickeyMinniePlutoHueyLouieDeweyDonaldGoofyWashington"

When asked why she had such a long password, she said she was told that it had to be at least 8 characters long and include at least one capital.

Contributed by Linda Anderson

A Pie in The Oven

6/16/2008

A woman was getting a homemade cherry pie ready to put into the oven when the phone rang. It was the school nurse. Her son had come down with a high fever, and would she come and take him home? The mother calculated how long it would take to drive to school and back, and how long the pie should bake, and concluded there was enough time. Popping the pie in the oven, she left for school. When she arrived, her son's fever was worse and the nurse urged her to take him to the doctor.

She drove to the clinic as fast as she dared. She was frayed a bit more as the doctor emerged from the examining room and handed her a slip of paper. "Get him to bed," he told her, handing her the prescription, "and start him on this right away."

By the time she got the boy home and in bed and headed out again for the shopping mall, she was not only frayed, but frazzled and frantic as well. And she had forgotten about the pie in the oven.

At the mall she found a pharmacy, got the prescription filled, and rushed back to the car, which was locked. There were her keys, hanging in the ignition switch, locked inside the car.

She began searching the mall for a wire coat hanger -- which turned out not to be easy. Wooden hangers and plastic hangers were there in abundance, but shops didn't use wire hangers anymore. After combing through a dozen stores, she finally found a wire hanger. Hurrying out of the mall, she halted. She stared at the wire coat hanger. "I don't know what to do with this!"

Then she remembered the pie in the oven. All the frustrations of the past hour collapsed on her and she began crying. Then she prayed, "Dear Lord, my boy is sick and he needs this medicine and my pie is in the oven and the keys are locked in the car. Lord, I don't know what to do with this coat hanger. Dear Lord, send somebody who does know what do with it, and I really need that person NOW, Lord. Amen."

She was wiping her eyes when a beat-up older car pulled up to the curb and stopped in front of her. A young man, twentyish-looking, in a stained T-shirt and ragged jeans, got out. He was coming her way. When he drew near, she stepped in front of him and held out the wire coat hanger. "Young man," she said, "do you know how to get into a locked car with one of these?"

He gaped at her for a moment and then plucked the hanger from her hand. "Where's the car?"

She had never seen anything like it -- it was simply amazing how easily he got into her car. A quick look at the door and window, a couple of twists of the coat hanger, and the door was open. When she saw that, she threw her arms around him.

"Oh," she said, "the Lord sent you! You're such a good boy."

He stepped back and said, "No, ma'am, I'm not a good boy. I just got out of prison yesterday for car theft."

She jumped at him and she hugged him again fiercely. "Bless the Lord!" she cried. "He sent me a professional!"

Contributed by Tom Benner

Please Warn the Pope

1/26/2006

Year 1981

1. Prince Charles got married
2. Liverpool crowned soccer Champions of Europe
3. Australia lost the Ashes tournament.
4. The Pope Died

Year 2005

1. Prince Charles got married
2. Liverpool crowned soccer Champions of Europe
3. Australia lost the Ashes tournament
4. The Pope Died

In the future, if Prince Charles decides to remarry ... please warn the Pope!

Contributed by Ron Heisler

Politically Correct Holiday Greetings

12-11-2006

"Please accept with no obligation, implied or implicit, our best wishes for an environmentally conscious, socially responsible, low-stress, non-addictive, gender-neutral celebration of the winter solstice holiday, practiced within the most enjoyable traditions of the religious persuasion of your choice or secular practices of your choice, with respect for the religious/secular persuasion and/or traditions of others, or their choice not to practice religious or secular traditions at all. We also wish you a fiscally successful, personally fulfilling and medically uncomplicated recognition of the generally accepted calendar year 2007 but with due respect for the calendars of choice of other cultures whose contributions to society have helped make America great. This is not to imply that America is necessarily greater than any other country nor the only America in the Western Hemisphere. This is also without regard to the race, creed, color, age, physical ability, religious faith or sexual preference of the wishes.

"By accepting these greetings you are accepting these terms. This greeting is subject to clarification or withdrawal. It is freely transferable with no alteration to the original greeting. It implies no promise by the wisher to actually implement any of the wishes for herself or himself or others, and is void where prohibited by law and is revocable at the sole discretion of the wisher. This wish is warranted to perform as expected within the usual application of good tidings for a period of one year or

until the issuance of a subsequent holiday greeting, whichever comes first, and warranty is limited to replacement of this wish or issuance of a new wish at the sole discretion of the wisher."

Bill Williams

Contributed by David Taylor

Proofreading Is a Dying Art

12/14/2009

Man Kills Self Before Shooting Wife and Daughter
This one I caught in the SGV Tribune the other day and called
the Editorial Room and asked who wrote this. It took two or
three readings before the editor realized that what he was reading
was impossible!!! They put in a correction the next day.

Something Went Wrong in Jet Crash, Expert Says
No crap, really? Ya think?

Police Begin Campaign to Run Down Jaywalkers
Now that's taking things a bit far!

Panda Mating Fails; Veterinarian Takes Over
What a guy!

Miners Refuse to Work after Death
No-good-for-nothing' lazy so-and-so's!

Juvenile Court to Try Shooting Defendant
See if that works any better than a fair trial!

War Dims Hope for Peace
I can see where it might have that effect!

If Strike Isn't Settled Quickly, It May Last Awhile
Ya think?!

Cold Wave Linked to Temperatures
Who would have thought!

London Couple Slain; Police Suspect Homicide

They may be on to something!

Red Tape Holds Up New Bridges
You mean there's something stronger than duct tape?

Man Struck By Lightning: Faces Battery Charge
He probably IS the battery charge!

New Study of Obesity Looks for Larger Test Group
Weren't they fat enough?

Astronaut Takes Blame for Gas in Spacecraft
That's what he gets for eating those beans!

Kids Make Nutritious Snacks
Do they taste like chicken?

Local High School Dropouts Cut in Half
Chainsaw Massacre all over again!

Hospitals are Sued by 7 Foot Doctors
Boy, are they tall!

Typhoon Rips Through Cemetery; Hundreds Dead
Did I read that right?

Contributed by Linda Anderson

Rare Blood Type!

5/3/2024

An Arab Sheik was admitted to Hospital for heart surgery but. prior to the surgery, the doctors needed to have some of his blood type stored in case the need arose.

As the gentleman had an extremely rare type of blood that couldn't be found locally, the call went out around the world.

Finally, a Scotsman was located who had the same rare blood type. After some coaxing, the Scot donated his blood for the Arab.

After the surgery, the Arab sent the Scotsman a new BMW, a diamond necklace for his wife, and $100,000 US dollars in appreciation for the blood donation.

A few months later, the Arab had to undergo a corrective surgery procedure. Once again, his doctor telephoned the Scotsman who this time was more than happy to donate his blood.

After the second surgery, the Arab sent the Scotsman a thank-you card and a box of Quality Street chocolates.

The Scotsman was shocked that the Arab did not reciprocate his kind gesture as he had anticipated. He then phoned the Arab and asked him: "I thought you would be more generous than that - last time you sent me a BMW, diamonds and money, but this time you only sent me a lousy thank-you card and a crappy box of chocolates?"

To this the Arab replied: "Aye laddie, but I now have Scottish blood in me veins."

Contributed by Judy Flahiff

Reporting a Missing Wife

9/15/2023

Husband: My wife is missing. She went shopping yesterday and hasn't come home.

Sergeant: How tall is she?

Husband: Gee, I'm not sure, a little over five-feet tall.

Sergeant: Weight?

Husband: Don't know. Not slim, not really fat.

Sergeant: Color of eyes?

Husband: Never noticed.

Sergeant: Color of hair?

Husband: Changes a couple times a year. Maybe dark brown.

Sergeant: What was she wearing?

Husband: Could have been a skirt or shorts. I don't remember exactly.

Sergeant: What kind of car did she go in?

Husband: She went in my truck.

Sergeant: What kind of truck was it?

Husband: Brand new Ford F150 King Ranch 4X4 with eco-boost 5.0L V8 engine special ordered with manual transmission. It has a custom matching white cover for the bed. Custom leather seats and "Bubba" floor mats. A Trailering package with gold hitch. DVD with navigation, 21-channel CB radio, six cup holders, and four power outlets. Added special alloy wheels and off-road Michelins. My wife put a small scratch on the driver's door…

At this point the husband started choking up.

Sergeant: Don't worry buddy. We'll find your truck.

Contributed by Ron Gargasz

Rules are Rules

3/24/2010

It was a normal day in Sharon Springs, Kansas when a Union Pacific crew boarded a loaded coal train for the long trek to Salina.

<u>The Bad news:</u>

Just a few miles into the trip, a wheel bearing became overheated and melted letting a metal support drop down and grind on the rail, creating white hot molten metal droppings spewing down to the rail.

<u>The Good news:</u>

A very alert crew noticed smoke about halfway back in the train and immediately stopped the train in compliance with the rules.

<u>The Bad news:</u>

The train stopped with the hot wheel over a wooden bridge with creosote ties and trusses. The crew tried to explain to higher-ups but were instructed not to move the train!

They were instructed to follow the <u>RULE</u> that prohibits moving the train when a part is defective!

RULES ARE RULES!

(Don't let common sense get in the way of a good disaster!)

Contributed by Bubba & Bonnie Mehling

A Senior's View of Electronics

9/23/2009

Things are spiraling out of control. I've become lost in a world of electronic madness.

One of my sons informed me this week that my cell phone has become obsolete and I should head down to the Cell Phone store to get a phone that is contemporary with the times. I pointed out that the fancy Razor/Slim-Line phone (with camera built in), that he made me trade my perfectly good flip-top Motorola cell phone for two years ago, still works perfectly fine. Well, except for the camera thing. Never could figure that part out. Even the few times I actually did take pictures, I couldn›t figure what to do with them. I just gave up, except for the times when I'd push the wrong button and take a video of the ceiling or my feet.

As for 'texting' ... I›m absolutely unable to text with the tiny little three-character buttons. "Hi, son," comes out looking like, "Gh Qmo." My grandkids have even spoken to my wife about "Poppa's crazy text messages." Give me a break. Whatever happened to actually talking on a phone? Isn't that what they were invented for?

Now, they want me to get one of those 'new' phones - the ones you can turn upside down and sideways. The ones with a typewriter keyboard..with keys about one-eighth the size of my pinky finger.

One of my four sons is a realtor whose real occupation is fly fishing. "Way to go, son." Or in my text language, "Xbz um Io, rmo."

We were floating the Yakima River in his guide quality drift boat south of Ellensburg, Washington. We were miles from anything remotely resembling civilization. Rock canyon walls were on either side of us. (Please bear with me as I try to explain this strange thing.) His "Blackberry" rang. It was blue, so I asked him why it wasn't called a

"Blueberry." He shook his head with that "dealing with an elder" look of despair. I get that look a lot these days. It was another realtor calling him to say that the sellers he represented had agreed to my son's client's changes and he had the signed documents in hand.

My son told him to FAX the papers to his office and he would get them signed and faxed back in order to close the deal that morning. A minute later the phone rang. He hit a few buttons and looked over the FAX which was now on the Yakima River with us.

He then called his clients and told them he was faxing the papers to them to sign and asked them to FAX them back to his office. While he was waiting, he hooked into a fat rainbow and was just releasing this 22-inch beauty as his phone rang again..with the signed FAX from his clients. He called the other realtor and told him he was sending the signed papers back by FAX. The deal was closed. My son then smiled and said.."You're a little behind the times Dad."

I guess I am. I thought about the sixty million dollar a year business I ran - with 1800 employees - all without a Blackberry that played music, took videos, still pictures, and communicated with Facebook & Twitter.

I signed up under duress for Twitter and Facebook so my seven kids, their spouses, my 13 grandkids and two great grandkids could all communicate with me in the modern way. I figured I could handle something as simple as Twitter with only 140 characters of space.

That was before one of my grandkids hooked me up for Tweeter, Tweetree, Twhirl, Twitterfon, Tweetie, Twittererific, Tweetdeck, Twitpix and something that sends every message to my cell phone and every other program within the texting world.

My phone was beeping every three minutes with the details of everything except the bowel movements of the entire next generation. I am not ready to live like this. I keep my cell phone in the garage in my golf bag.

The kids bought me a GPS for my last birthday because they say I get lost every now and then going over to the grocery store or the library. I keep that in a box under my tool bench with the Bluetooth [it's red] phone I'm supposed to use when I drive. I wore it once, and was standing in line at Barnes and Noble, talking to my wife.

Suddenly I realized everyone within 50 yards was glaring at me. Seems I had to take my hearing aid out, to use my Bluetooth and I'd gotten a little loud.

The GPS thingie did look pretty smart on my dashboard but the lady inside was the most annoying and rudest person I'd run into in a long while. Every 10 minutes, she'd sarcastically say, "Re-calc-ul-ating." You'd think she could be a bit nicer. It seemed like she could barely tolerate me. She'd let go with a deep sigh and then tell me to make a U-turn at the next light. Then, when I'd make a right turn instead .. well, it was not good.

When I get really lost now, I call my wife and tell her the name of the cross streets - and while she's starting to develop the same tone as "Gypsy," the GPS lady, at least she loves me!

To be perfectly frank, I'm still trying to learn how to use the cordless phones in our house. We have had them for four years and I still haven't figured out how I can lose all three phones at once and then have to dig under chair cushions, check bathrooms, and the dirty laundry basket whenever the phone rings. (I did find my glasses case and the extra TV remote.)

The world is just getting too complex for me. They even mess me up every time I go to the grocery store. You'd think they could settle on something themselves, but this "Paper or Plastic?" thing, every time I check out, just knocks me for a loop. I bought some of those cloth, re-usable, bags to avoid looking confused - but I never remember to take them in with me.

Now I just toss it back at 'em. When they ask me, "Paper or Plastic?" I simply say, "Doesn't matter to me. I'm 'bi-sacksual'." Then it's their turn to stare at me with a blank look!

Contributed by Julius Graw

Setting an Example

6/8/2009

His name was Jim. He had wild hair, wore a T-shirt with holes in it, jeans, and no shoes. This was literally his wardrobe for his entire four years of college. He was brilliant. Kind of profound and very, very bright.

Across the street from the campus was a well-dressed, very conservative church. They wanted to develop a ministry to the students but were not sure how to go about it.

One day Jim decided to go there. He walked in with no shoes, jeans, his T-shirt, and wild hair. The service had already started and so Jim started down the aisle looking for a seat.

The church was completely packed and he couldn't find a seat. By now, people were really looking a bit uncomfortable, but no one said anything.

Jim got closer and closer and closer to the pulpit and, when he realized that there were no seats, he just squatted down right on the carpet.

By now the people were really uptight and the tension in the air was thick.

About this time, the minister realized that, from way at the back of the church, a deacon was slowly making his way toward Jim.

Now the deacon was in his eighties, had silver-gray hair, and wore a three-piece suit. A godly man, very elegant, very dignified, very courtly, he walked with a cane and, as he started walking toward this boy, everyone was saying to themselves that you couldn't blame him for what he was going to do. How can you expect a man of his age and of his background to understand some college kid on the floor?

It took a long time for the man to reach the boy.

The church was utterly silent except for the clicking of the man's cane. All eyes were focused on him. You couldn't even hear anyone breathing and the minister couldn't even continue the sermon until the deacon did what he had to do.

And then they saw this elderly man drop his cane on the floor. With great difficulty, he lowered himself and sat down next to Jim and worshiped with him so he wouldn't be alone.

Everyone choked up with emotion. When the minister gained control, he said, "What I'm about to preach, you won't remember. What you have just seen, you'll never forget. Be careful how you live. You may be the only Bible some people will ever read!"

Contributed by David Hoiles

Singing in Church

8/8/2006

A minister decided to do something a little different one Sunday morning. He said "Today I am going to say a series of single words and you're going to guide the service. Whatever single word I say, I want you to sing whatever hymn that comes to your mind."

The minister shouted out "CROSS."

Immediately the congregation started singing in unison, "THE OLD RUGGED CROSS."

The minister hollered out "GRACE" and the congregation began to sing "AMAZING GRACE, how sweet the sound."

The pastor said "POWER" and the congregation sang "THERE IS POWER IN THE BLOOD."

But when the Pastor said "SEX," the congregation fell into total silence. Everyone was in shock. They all nervously began to look around at each other afraid to say anything.

Then all of a sudden, way from in the back of the church, a little old 87-year-old grandmother stood up and began to sing "PRECIOUS MEMORIES."

Contributed by David Taylor

Sometimes Seniors Don't Understand Directions

12/28/2023

If you're a Senior, you should listen to your doctor's instructions.

I went to my nearby CVS Pharmacy, straight to the back where the Pharmacists' high counter is located.

I took out my little brown bottle, along with a teaspoon, and set them up on the counter.

The Pharmacist came over, smiled, and asked if he could help me.

I said, "Yes! Could you please <u>taste</u> this for me?"

Seeing a senior citizen, the Pharmacist went along.

He took the spoon, put a tiny bit of the liquid on it, put it on his tongue and swilled it around.

Then, with a stomach-churning look on his face, he spat it out on the floor and began coughing.

When he finally was finished, I looked him right in the eye and asked, "Now, does that <u>taste</u> sweet to you?"

The Pharmacist, shaking his head back and forth with a venomous look in his eyes yelled, "HELL NO!!!"

I said, "Oh, thank God! That's a real relief! My doctor told me to have a pharmacist test my urine for sugar!"

I can never go back to that CVS, but I really don't care, because they aren't very friendly there anymore!

Contributed by David Taylor

Sounds Like He's Self-Employed

10/11/2006

A man owned a small ranch in Nevada. The Nevada Department of Labor claimed he was not paying proper wages to his help and sent an agent out to interview him. "I need a list of your employees and how much you pay them," demanded the agent.

"Well," replied the rancher, "There's my ranch hand who's been with me for three years. I pay him $600 a week plus free room and board. The cook has been here for 18 months, and I pay her $500 per week plus free room and board. Then there's the half-wit who works here about 18 hours every day and does about 90% of all the work around here. He makes $10 per week, and I buy him a bottle of bourbon every Saturday night."

"That's the guy I want to talk to -- the half-wit," said the agent.

"That would be me," replied the rancher.

Contributed by Ron Heisler

Southern Professional Engineers' Exam

7/21/2006

(We are sick and tired of hearing about how dumb people in the South are. We challenge any so-called smart Yankee to take this exam administered by the Southern States Professional Engineer Licensing Authority:)

1. Calculate the smallest limb diameter on a persimmon tree that will support a 10-pound possum.
2. Which of these cars will rust out the quickest when placed on blocks in your front yard? A) '65 Ford Fairlane, B) '69 Chevrolet, C) '67 Chevelle, or D) '64 Pontiac GTO.
3. If your uncle builds a still that operates at a capacity of 20 gallons of shine produced per hour, how many car radiators are required to condense the product?
4. A woodcutter has a chain saw that operates at 2700 RPM. The density of the pine trees in the plot to be harvested is 470 per acre. The plot is 2.3 acres in size. The average tree diameter is 14 inches. How many Budweisers will be drunk before the trees are cut down?
5. If every old refrigerator in the state vented a charge of R-12 simultaneously, what would be the percentage decrease in the ozone layer?
6. A front porch is constructed of 2x8 pine on 24-inch centers with a field rock foundation. The span is 8 feet and the porch length is 16 feet. The porch floor is 1-inch rough sawn pine. When the porch collapses, how many hound dogs will be killed?
7. A man owns a Tennessee house and 3.7 acres of land in a hollow with an average slope of 15%. The man has five children. Can each

of his grown children put a mobile home on the man's land and still have enough property for their electric appliances to sit out front?

8. A 2-ton truck is overloaded and proceeding 9000 yards down a steep slope on a secondary road at 45 MPH. The brakes fail. Given average traffic conditions on secondary roads, what is the probability that it will strike a vehicle that is insured?

9. A coal mine operates in a NFPA Class 1, Division 2 Hazardous Area. The mine employs 120 miners per shift. A gas warning is issued at the beginning of the 3rd shift. How many cartons of unfiltered Camels will be smoked during the shift?

10. At a reduction in the gene pool variability rate of 7.5% per generation, how long will it take a town that has been bypassed by the Interstate to breed a country-western singer?

Good Luck - You have three hours for the exam.

Contributed by Bubba Mehling

Stories To Remind You of Wiley Coyote

10/24/2024

Think you're having a bad day?

Fire authorities in California found a corpse in a burned-out section of forest while assessing the damage done by a forest fire. The deceased male was dressed in a full wet suit, complete with scuba tanks on his back, flippers, and face mask. A postmortem test revealed that the man died not from burns, but from massive internal injuries. Dental records provided a positive identification.

Investigators then set about to determine how a fully clothed diver ended up in the middle of a forest fire. It was revealed that on the day of the fire, the man went diving off the coast, some 20 miles from the forest. The fire fighters, seeking to control the fire as quickly as possible, had called in a fleet of helicopters with very large dip buckets. Water was dipped from the ocean and emptied at the site of the forest fire. You guessed it. One minute our diver was making like Flipper in the Pacific, the next, he was doing the breaststroke in a fire dip bucket 300 feet in the air. Some days it just doesn't pay to get out of bed but keep reading...

Still think you're having a bad day?

A man was working on his motorcycle on the patio, his wife nearby in the kitchen. While racing the engine, the motorcycle accidentally slipped into gear. The man, still holding onto the handlebars, was dragged along as it burst through the glass patio doors.

His wife, hearing the crash, ran in the room to find her husband cut and bleeding, the motorcycle, and the shattered patio door. She called for an ambulance and, because the house sat on a fairly large hill, went down several flights of stairs to meet the paramedics and escort them to her husband.

While the attendants were loading her husband, the wife managed to right the motorcycle and push it outside. She also quickly blotted up the spilled petrol with some paper towels and tossed them into the toilet.

After being treated and released, the man returned home, looked at the shattered patio door and the damage done to his motorcycle. He went into the bathroom and consoled himself with a cigarette while attending to his business. About to stand, he flipped the butt between his legs.

The wife, who was in the kitchen, heard a loud explosion and her husband screaming. Finding him lying on the bathroom floor with his trousers blown away and burns on his buttocks, legs and groin, she once again phoned for an ambulance.

The same paramedic crew was dispatched. As the paramedics carried the man down the stairs to the ambulance, they asked the wife how he had come to burn himself. She told them. They started laughing so hard, one slipped, the stretcher dumping the husband out. He fell down the remaining stairs, breaking his arm.

Still having a bad day? Just remember, it could be worse.

The average cost of rehabilitating a seal after the Exxon Valdez oil spill in Alaska was $80,000. At a special ceremony, two of the most expensively saved animals were being released back into the wild amid cheers and applause from onlookers. A minute later, in full view, a killer whale ate them both.

Still think you're having a bad day?

A woman came home to find her husband in the kitchen shaking frantically, almost in a dancing frenzy, with some kind of wire running from his waist towards the electric kettle.

Intending to jolt him away from the deadly current, she whacked him with a handy plank of wood, breaking his arm in two places. Up to that moment, he had been happily listening to his Walkman.

STILL think you're having a bad day?

Two animal rights protesters were protesting at the cruelty of sending pigs to a slaughterhouse in Bonn, Germany. Suddenly, all two thousand pigs broke loose and escaped through a broken fence, stampeding madly. The two hapless protesters were trampled to death.

What? STILL having a bad day?

Iraqi terrorist Khay Rahnajet didn't pay enough postage on a letter bomb. It came back with 'return to sender' stamped on it. Forgetting it was the bomb, he opened it and was blown to bits.
There now, feeling better?

Contributed by Tod Butler

Taking Aim at Cheney

2/24/2006

AFTER THE RECENT HUNTING INCIDENT IN TEXAS,
HERE ARE SOME OF THE NEWSPAPER HEADLINES.

<u>Kingsville Dispatch</u>
"Game Warden Fines Cheney $100 For Only Wounding Lawyer"

<u>National Review</u> Online
"Red States Poll Shows Cheney Shooting Was Justifiable"

<u>San Antonio Express/News</u>
"Sneaky Lawyer Tactics Don't Work on Cheney"

<u>LUBBOCK AVALANCHE JOURNAL</u>
"Cheney Sends Message to Terrorist"

<u>POST TRIBUNE</u>
"Cheney Said He Tried to Get Special Forces to Take Him Out"

LONGVIEW GAZETTE
"Tom Delay Had Lawyer Fill His Slot for
Last Minute Hunting Trip with VP"

STEPHENVILLE EMPIRE
Cheney Quoted - "You Should Have Seen the One That Got Away"

WICHITA FALLS TIMES HERALD
"Cheney adds new meaning to Tourist Season!"

CHILDRESS TRIBUNE
"LAWYER SHOT ONCE, OFFICIALS SAY GUN JAMMED"

WEATHERFORD DEMOCRAT
"Lawyer Used as Decoy"

USA TODAY
"Cheney In Texas Promoting Republicans' New Medical Plan?"

SAN ANGELO TIMES
"Cheney Now Seen as Major Threat for Presidential Bid"

NRA American Rifleman
"Witnesses Claim Cheney Only Feathered Lawyer"

AMERICAN SPORTSMAN
Guide Claims Cheney Misunderstood, "I said, 'Condoleezza
Rice,' NOT 'Quick, Lawyer to Your RIGHT!'"

KERRVILLE PRESS
"Cheney Didn't have Proper Hunting License or Lawyer Stamp"

BASTROP AMERICAN
"Cheney Testing State's New Tort Reform"

GEORGETOWN NEWS
"Cheney Invites Hillary Clinton to Deer Hunting Trip"

WACO TIMES
"Cheney Shoots Austin Lawyer - "Cheney Popularity Approval Rating Now Standing at 98%"

Dallas Morning News
"Shot Came from Grassy Knoll"

Austin Statesman
"Cheney Says Victim's Quail Call Was Best He Ever Heard"

Washington Post
"Cheney Prevents Hunting Party from Field Dressing Shooting Victim"

The Nation
"Cheney Drove Shooting Victim to Hospital Tied to The Hood of His Car"

<u>Houston Chronicle</u>
***"Personal Injury Lawyers Hold Candlelight
Vigil Outside Cheney Victim Hospital"***

<u>Wyoming Tribune Eagle</u>
"Cheney Friends Decline Fall Duck Hunting Invitation"

<u>La Raza</u>
***"Cheney Shooting Victim Gets Emergency
Room Priority Over Illegal Aliens!"***

<u>Vegan News</u>
"Cheney Shooting Victim Converts to Vegetarian in Hospital"

The Texas Parks and Wildlife Department issued a statement today saying Vice President Cheney broke no law by shooting a lawyer instead of a quail over the weekend.

A TPWD spokesman noted that in Texas lawyers are not considered wild game and are thus not subject to seasonal limits. It was further noted that the extermination of lawyers was encouraged as the state is being overrun with these pests. The TWPD briefly considered selling "lawyer tags" in the early 70's when the population exploded, but the measure was not introduced after the Texas Bar Association threatened suit.

A local food critic said that, contrary to rumor, lawyers do not taste like chicken, but rather like bull****.

Contributed by Julius Graw and David Taylor

Texas Fun Facts

11/27/2009

Beaumont to El Paso: 742 miles; Beaumont to Chicago: 770 miles

World's first rodeo was in Pecos, Texas on July 4, 1883.

The Flagship Hotel in Galveston is the only hotel in North America built over water.

The Heisman Trophy was named after John William Heisman who was the first full time coach for Rice University, Houston.

Brazoria County has more species of birds than any other area in North America. Aransas Wildlife Refuge is the winter home of North America's only remaining flock of whooping cranes.

Jalapeno jelly originated in Lake Jackson in 1978.

The worst natural disaster in U.S. history was in 1900 caused by a hurricane in which over 8000 lives were lost on Galveston Island.

The first word spoken from the moon, July 20, 1969, was "Houston."

El Paso is closer to California than to Dallas.

Laredo is the world's largest inland port.

Tyler Municipal Rose Garden is the world's largest rose garden with over 38,000 bushes with 500 varieties on 22 acres.

The State shell is Lightning Whelk.

The King Ranch is larger than Rhode Island.

Tropical Storm Claudette brought a U.S. rainfall record of 43" in 24 hours in and around Alvin in July 1979.

Texas is the only state to enter the U.S. by TREATY, instead of by annexation. (This allows the Texas flag to fly at the same height as the US flag.)

A Live Oak tree near Fulton is estimated to be 1500 years old.

Caddo Lake is the only natural lake in the state.

Dr Pepper was invented in Waco in 1885. There is no period after Dr in Dr Pepper.

Texas has had six capital cities.

1. Washington-on-the-Brazos
2. Harrisburg
3. Galveston
4. Velasco
5. West Columbia
6. Austin

The Capitol Dome in Austin is the only dome in the U.S. which is taller than the Capitol Building in Washington D.C. by seven feet.

The name Texas comes from the Hasini Indian word "tejas" meaning friends. Tejas is not Mexican for Texas.

The first domed stadium in the U.S. was the Astrodome in Houston.

The State animal is the Armadillo. An interesting bit of trivia about the armadillo is they always have four babies! They have one egg which splits into four and they either have four males or four females.

Contributed by Susan Luna

"I Don't Care! That's What the Plans Said!!!"

9/9/2009

From the "Does Anybody have a half a brain" department...

ЦЕНТР ПРОДАЖ

W.G. Williams

Contributed by Sherry Niese

The Difference

2/2/2007

In the light of the increased frequency of human/grizzly bear conflicts, the Alaska Dept of Fish & Game is advising tourists, hikers, and fishermen to take extra care and keep alert for bears whilst traveling this summer.

They advise people to wear noisy little bells on their clothing so as not to startle bears that are not expecting them. They also advise everyone to carry pepper spray with them in case they encounter a grizzly.

It's also a good idea to watch out for fresh signs of bear activity. Outdoorsmen should recognize the difference between black bear and grizzly bear dung.

Black bear dung is smaller and contains berries and squirrel fur. Grizzly bear dung has little bells in it and smells like pepper.

Contributed by David Taylor

The Goat

1/4/2010

Two guys were out hunting and, as they walked along, they came upon a huge hole in the ground. They approached and were amazed by the size of it. The first hunter said, "Wow, that's some hole; I can't even see the bottom. I wonder how deep it is."

The second replied, "I don't know. Let's throw something down and listen and see how long it takes to hit bottom."

"I saw an old automobile transmission back a ways. Give me a hand and we'll throw it in and see."

They picked it up and carried it over, counted one and two and three, and threw it into the hole.

As they were standing there listening and looking over the edge, they heard a rustling in the brush behind them. As they turned around, they saw a goat come crashing through the brush. It ran up to the hole and, with no hesitation, jumped in headfirst.

While they were standing there looking at each other, looking in the hole, and trying to figure out what that was all about, an old farmer walked up. "Say there," said the farmer, "you fellers didn't happen to see my goat around here anywhere, did you?"

The first hunter said, " Funny you should ask, but we were just standing here a minute ago and a goat came running out of the bushes doin' about a hunert miles an hour and jumped headfirst into this hole here!"

The old farmer said "Why that's impossible! I had him chained to an old transmission!"

Contributed by Linda Narges

The Hairdresser

10/6/2011

This is something to think about when negative people are doing their best to rain on your parade. Remember this story the next time someone who knows nothing and cares less, tries to make your life miserable.

A woman was at her hairdresser's getting her hair styled for a trip to Rome with her husband. She mentioned the trip to the hairdresser, who responded, "Rome? Why would anyone want to go there? It's crowded and dirty. You're crazy to go to Rome. So, how are you getting there?"

"We're taking Continental," was the reply. "We got a great rate!"

"Continental?" exclaimed the hairdresser. "That's a terrible airline. Their planes are old, their flight attendants are ugly, and they're always late. So, where are you staying in Rome?"

"We'll be at this exclusive little place over on Rome's Tiber River called Teste."

"Don't go any further. I know that place. Everybody thinks it's gonna be something special and exclusive, but it's really a dump, the worst hotel in the city! The rooms are small, the service is surly, and they are overpriced. So, whatcha' doing when you get there?"

"We're going to go to see the Vatican and we hope to see the Pope."

"That's rich," laughed the hairdresser. "You and a million other people are trying to see him. He'll look the size of an ant. Boy, good luck on this lousy trip of yours. You're going to need it."

A month later, the woman again came in for a hairdo. The hairdresser asked her about her trip to Rome.

"It was wonderful," explained the woman. "Not only were we on time in one of Continental's brand-new planes but it was over-booked and they bumped us up to first class. The food and wine were wonderful, and I had a handsome 28-year-old steward who waited on me hand and foot.

"And the hotel was great! They'd just finished a $5 million remodeling job and now it's a jewel … the finest hotel in the city. They, too were overbooked, so they apologized and gave us their owner's suite at no extra charge!"

"Well," muttered the hairdresser, "that's all well and good, but I know you didn't get to see the Pope."

"Actually, we were quite lucky because, as we toured the Vatican, a Swiss Guard tapped me on the shoulder and explained that the Pope likes to meet some of the visitors and, if I'd be so kind as to step into his private room and wait, the Pope would personally greet me.

"Sure enough, five minutes later, the Pope walked through the door and shook my hand. I knelt down and he spoke a few words to me."

"Oh, really! What'd he say?"

"The Pope said, "Where'd you get that terrible hairdo?""

Contributed by Bubba & Bonnie Mehling

The Next War

3/21/2007

At the Russian War College, a general was a guest lecturer and told the class of officers that the session would focus on potential problems and the resulting strategies.

One of the officers in the class began by asking, "Will we have to fight in a third world war?"

"Yes, comrades, it looks like you will," answered the general.

"And who will be our primary enemy, Comrade General?" another officer asked.

"The likelihood is that it will be China."

The class was surprised and finally one officer asked, "But Comrade General, we are 150 million people, and they are about 1.5 billion. How can we possibly win?"

"Well," replied the general, "Think about it. In modern war, it is not quantity but quality that is the key. For example, in the Middle East, five million Jews have been fighting against 50 million Arabs, and the Jews have been the winners every time."

"But sir," asked the panicky officer, "We don't have enough Jews!"

Contributed by Julius Graw

The Old Timers' Bar

1/6/2010

Four guys were walking down a street in The Villages, Florida. They turned a corner and saw a sign that said, "Old Timers Bar - all drinks 10 cents." They looked at each other, and then went in thinking, "This is too good to be true."

The old bartender said in a voice that carries across the room, "Come on in and let me pour one for you! What'll it be, Gentlemen?"

There seemed to be a fully stocked bar, so each of the men asked for a martini. In short order, the bartender served up four iced martinis... shaken, not stirred, and said, "That'll be 10 cents each, please."

They stared at the bartender for a moment then looked at each other in amazement ... they couldn't believe their good luck.

They paid the 40 cents, finished their martinis, and ordered another round. Again, four excellent martinis were produced with the bartender again saying, "That's 40 cents, please."

They paid the 40 cents, but their curiosity was more than they can stand. They have each had two martinis and so far, they've spent less than a dollar.

Finally, one of the men says, "How can you afford to serve martinis as good as these for a dime apiece?"

"I'm a retired tailor from Boston," the bartender said, "and I always wanted to own a bar. Last year I hit the Lottery for $25 million and decided to open this place. Every drink costs a dime - wine, liquor, beer, it's all the same."

"Wow!!!! That's quite a story," said one of the men.

The four of them sipped at their martinis and couldn't help but notice seven other people at the end of the bar who didn't have drinks in front of them and hadn't ordered anything the whole time they were there.

One man gestured at the seven at the end of the bar without drinks and asks the bartender, "What's with them?"

The bartender replied, "Oh, they're all old, retired farts from Texas waiting for happy hour when drinks are half price."

Contributed by Ron Gargasz

The "Rules"

10/26/2010

We always hear "the rules" from the female side;
now here are the rules from the male side.

These are our rules! (Please note... these are all numbered "1" ON PURPOSE!

1. Men are NOT mind readers. (FIRST & FOREMOST RULE)

1. Learn to work the toilet seat. You're a big girl. If it's up, put it down. We need it up, you need it down. You don't hear us complaining about you leaving it down.

1. Sunday sports, they're like the full moon or the changing of the tides. Let it be.

1. Crying is blackmail.

1. Ask for what you want. Let us be clear on this one: Subtle hints do not work! Strong hints do not work! Obvious hints do not work! Just say it!

1. Yes and No are perfectly acceptable answers to almost every question

1. Come to us with a problem only if you want help solving it. That's what we do. Sympathy is what your girlfriends are for.

1. Anything we said 6 months ago is inadmissible in an argument. In fact, all comments become null and void after 7 days.

1. If you think you're fat, you probably are. Don't ask us.

1. If something we said can be interpreted two ways and one of the ways makes you sad or angry, we meant the other one.

1. You can either ask us to do something or tell us how you want it done. Not both. If you already know best how to do it, just do it yourself.

1. Whenever possible, please say whatever you have to say during commercials.

1. Christopher Columbus didn't need directions and neither do we.

1. ALL men see in only 16 colors, like Windows default settings. Peach, for example, is a fruit, not a color. Pumpkin is also a fruit. We have no idea what mauve is.

1. If it itches, it will be scratched. We do that.

1. If we ask what is wrong and you say "nothing," We will act like nothing's wrong. We know you're lying, but it's just not worth the hassle.

1. If you ask a question you don't want an answer to, expect an answer you don't want to hear.

1. When we have to go somewhere, absolutely anything you wear is fine… Really!

1. Don't ask us what we're thinking about unless you are prepared to discuss such topics as Football or Hockey.

1. You have enough clothes.

1. You have too many shoes.

1. I am in shape. Round IS a shape!

1. Thank you for reading this. (Yes, I know, I'll have to sleep on the couch tonight; but did you know men really don't mind that? It's like camping.)

Contributed by Tim Butler

The Shoe Box

11/28/2007

A man and woman had been married for more than 60 years. They had shared everything. They had talked about everything. They had kept no secrets from each other except that the little old woman had a shoe box in the top of her closet that she had cautioned her husband never to open or ask her about. For all of these years, he had never thought about the box.

One day his wife got very sick and the doctor said she would not recover.

In trying to sort out their affairs, the man took down the shoe box and took it to his wife's bedside. She agreed that it was time that he should know what was in the box.

When he opened it, he found two crocheted dolls and a stack of money totaling $95,000. He asked her about the contents.

"When we were to be married," she said, "my grandmother told me the secret of a happy marriage was to never argue. She told me that if I ever got angry with you, I should just keep quiet and crochet a doll."

The little old man was so moved; he had to fight back tears. Only two precious dolls were in the box. He thought she had only been angry with him twice in all those years of living and loving. He almost burst with happiness.

"Honey," he said, "that explains the dolls, but what about all of this money? Where did it come from?"

"Oh," she said, "that's what I made from selling the dolls."

Contributed by Ron Heisler

The Silent Thanksgiving

12/9/2025
From Facebook

Mike, who lives in Chicago, thinks I'm spending Thanksgiving with my daughter Sarah.

My Daughter Sarah, who's an ER nurse here in town, thinks I'm flying out to be with Mike.

The truth? It's 1:00 PM on Thanksgiving Day. I'm 79 years old, living in a quiet house outside Pittsburgh. And I just set the table for one.

My name is Frank. I poured steel at the mill for forty-five years. I've seen strikes that split this town in two, I've seen presidents come and go, and I've seen my kids grow up and move on. My wife Maria has been gone for six years. Six long Thanksgivings.

When she was alive, this day started at 6 AM. The house would fill up with the smell of roasting turkey and her sage stuffing by 9 AM. The Macy's parade would be glaring on the TV. I'd be tasked with mashing the potatoes, and I'd always make a mess, and she'd swat me with a dish towel, laughing. The house felt full. It felt alive.

This year the house is so quiet I can hear the pipes creak.

The calls came first. "Dad, it's chaos at O'Hare. They're forecasting a blizzard, and Janie's got that cough again. We just can risk the flight. You're going to Sarah's, right? You have a great time!"

I looked at the framed photo of his family on the mantel. "You bet, son. Don't you worry about me. You keep those kids warm. I'll be fine at your sister's."

Then Sarah called, her voice already tired. "Dad, they've cut our holiday staff again. It's going to be a warzone in the ER. I have to pull a double shift. I'm so sorry. But you're going to Mike's, aren't you? Thank God. Give the grandkids a huge hug from me."

I looked out the window at the empty driveway. "Of course, sweetheart. You go take care of people. I'm proud of you. I'll be fine with your brother."

The lies didn't even feel like lies. They felt … easier. Easier than saying the truth: "Please. Don't leave me alone. I don't want to be alone."

You spend your whole life being their rock, being the guy who fixes the bike and balances the checkbook. You forget how to tell them that you're crumbling.

Thanksgiving morning, I woke up before the sun. Habit. I made my coffee and sat at the kitchen table. The silence was deafening. Even my old beagle, Buddy, just slept in his bed, like he knew the day didn't matter.

"We've gotta do something," I told him. I remembered Maria had an old porcelain turkey platter. The one we only used for this day. She kept it on the top shelf of the pantry.

I grabbed the old wooden stepladder. The one with the wobbly leg I'd been meaning to fix for a decade.

I was on the top step, I know, not smart. I'm 79, not 29. I was reaching, my fingers just brushing the cold ceramic, when the step didn't just wobble. It snapped.

I fell backwards. Time slowed down. My head missed the corner of the counter by an inch. I landed flat on my back on the hard linoleum. The wind was punched clean out of me. The platter shattered on the floor next to me, into a hundred white pieces.

I just lay there. Staring at the ceiling. I couldn't breathe. I couldn't move.

My first thought wasn't about the pain. It was: "This is it. This is how they find you. A day from now. Maybe two. When the calls go unanswered."

Buddy scrambled over, whining, licking my face, frantic. His panic was like a jolt of electricity. "Alright boy," I wheezed, the words catching in my throat. "I'm not done yet."

It took me ten minutes to get to my knees. My hip was screaming. My hands were shaking so hard I couldn't grip the counter. When I finally pulled myself up, I wasn't just an old man anymore. I was an old man who was totally and completely alone.

I skipped the turkey. I swept up the broken pieces and threw them in the trash. I made myself a ham sandwich on white bread.

At 3:00 PM, my phone buzzed. A video call. It was Mike.

His face popped up, smiling, kids yelling in the background. "Hey Dad! How's Sarah's place? Is the food good? Put her on, I want to say hi!"

I hadn't planned this. My camera was pointed right at my empty kitchen. At my single plate. At my ham sandwich.

"She's … in the kitchen, son," I stammered.

"Well, yell for her!" he laughed.

Mike's wife, Karen, appeared over his shoulder. "Frank! Let me see the table! Did Sarah make her famous green bean casserole?"

I saw them see it. The way my kitchen was dark. The way the table behind me was empty, except for one plate.

Mike's smile didn't just fade. It fell.

"Dad … where is Sarah? He asked, his voice quiet.

I couldn't lie anymore. "She's at the hospital, Mike. She's working a double."

"Then … where are you?"

"I'm at home, son. It's fine. I just …"

"You're alone?"

His face went pale. I could see the realization hit him like a physical blow. He didn't know I could hear him yell to his wife, "He's alone! He's been alone all day. He lied to us!"

Before I could say, "Don't be silly," the call ended.

I sat there in silence feeling ashamed. Like I'd been caught. I turned on the TV. A football game. The announcer was yelling about something. I didn't care.

Hours later it was dark. Buddy started barking, a real, frantic bark.

Headlights sliced through the living room window. A car door slammed. Then another.

I pulled myself up, my hip throbbing, and went to the front door.

It was Sarah's little hatchback, and Mike's rented SUV.

Sarah didn't say anything. She just walked past me, dropped her bag, and hugged me so hard I thought my ribs would crack. She buried her face in my old flannel shirt. "I'm so sorry, Dad. I'm so, so sorry!"

Mike came in behind her. He was carrying a foil pan. "We're idiots," he said, his voice thick. "We're just idiots. We're here."

His kids, half-asleep, wrapped their arms around my legs.

We crowded around that old kitchen table. We pulled out chairs from the dining room. Mike's pan was lukewarm stuffing from his interrupted dinner. Karen had grabbed a half-eaten pumpkin pie. Sarah had stopped for a bucket of chicken on the way from the hospital.

We ate cold chicken and lukewarm stuffing off paper plates. My grandkids fell asleep on the sofa. We talked. We really talked. It was the best Thanksgiving I've ever had.

Here's what I learned last night, and what I wish every grown child could feel deep in their bones: "We, your parents, are from a generation that doesn't know how to ask for help. We'll say, 'I'm fine' and 'Don't make a fuss' until our very last breath. We'd rather eat a ham sandwich alone than make you feel guilty."

Your job is to know that we're lying.

Your job is to ask again. Your job is to call your siblings and check.

So, if you mom or dad sounds a little too "okay" this holiday … or any day … call their bluff! Turn the car around. Show up late. Bring leftovers. Bring a bucket of chicken. It doesn't matter.

Because these houses get silent. These bones get brittle. And one day, you'll give anything in the world to break that silence, to sit at that table just one more time … and you won't be able to!

Don't wait!

Don't wait! -- Show up for the ones you love!

W.G. Williams

The Start

11/25/2010

The Pilgrims came to America, an unsettled land,
To create a new life and to make a stand.
For freedom of spirit, of soul, and of mind,
Fearless as to what hazards they would find.
No hotels for shelter, or restaurants for food,
No theaters or concerts to lighten one's mood.
The vacant land challenged life itself.
There were no "How To" books on the shelf.
The necessity to face the task of personal survival
Became an immediate challenge on their arrival.
Their shelter was hewn from quickly felled trees,
Assembled out of necessity, not architecture to please.
Carefully stored seeds were planted with care
In trust of the good food the plants would bear.
Nature responded to meet their needs, and more,
With surplus from the harvest for the winter to store.
The excesses were turned into commodities for sale
Which provides a fitting ending to this amazing tale.
Now other people feeling safe and secure

Came to America with less hardship to endure.
Many felt a need to pause and openly rejoice
That God had rendered them a choice.
A Thanksgiving feast along with their Indian friends
Began a tradition which we trust will never end.

HAPPY THANKSGIVING

W.G. Williams

The Test

9/2/2005

While researching a story on mental asylums, a reporter asked the Director he was interviewing what the criteria was that defines whether a patient was to be institutionalized or not.

"Well," said the Director, "we often use logic. For example, we might fill up a bathtub, make a teaspoon, a teacup, and a bucket available to the patient and ask the patient to empty the bathtub."

"Oh, I understand," said the reporter. "A normal person would choose the bucket since it was larger than the spoon or the cup."

"Noooooo," answered the Director. "A normal person would pull the plug."

Contributed by Julius Graw

Things I've Learned from Bringing Up Boys:

8/29/2005

1.) A king size waterbed holds enough water to fill a 2000 sq. ft. house four inches deep.
2.) If you spray hair spray on dust bunnies and run over them with roller blades, they can ignite.
3.) A 3-year-old boy's voice is louder than 200 adults in a crowded restaurant.
4.) If you hook a dog leash over a ceiling fan, the motor is not strong enough to rotate 42-pound Boy wearing Batman underwear and a Superman cape. It is strong enough, however, if tied to a paint can, to spread paint on all four walls of a 20x20 ft. room.
5.) You should not throw baseballs up when the ceiling fan is on. When using a ceiling fan as a bat, you have to throw the ball up a few times before you get a hit. A ceiling fan can hit a baseball a long way.
6.) The glass in windows (even double pane) doesn't stop a baseball hit by a ceiling fan.
7.) When you hear the toilet flush and the words "uh oh," it's already too late.
8.) Brake fluid mixed with Clorox makes smoke, and lots of it.
9.) A six-year-old Boy can start a fire with a flint rock even though a 36-year-old man says they can only do it in the movies.
10.) Certain Lego's will pass through the digestive tract of a 4-year-old boy.
11.) Play dough and microwave should not be used in the same sentence.
12.) Super glue is forever.

13.) No matter how much Jell-O you put in a swimming pool you still can't walk on water.

14.) Pool filters do not like Jell-O.

15.) VCR's do not eject "PB &J" sandwiches even though TV commercials show they do.

16.) Garbage bags do not make good parachutes.

17.) Marbles in gas tanks make lots of noise when driving.

18.) You probably DO NOT want to know what that odor is.

19.) Always look in the oven before you turn it on; plastic toys do not like ovens.

20.) The fire department in Austin, TX has a 5-minute response time.

21.) The spin cycle on the washing machine does not make earthworms dizzy.

22.) It will, however, make cats dizzy.

23.) Cats throw up twice their body weight when dizzy.

24.) 80% of men who read this will try mixing the Clorox and brake fluid.

Contributed by Jamie Gillett

To All My Friends Who Have Mothers

In each human heart is that one special corner
Which only a mother can fill.

A mother is someone to shelter and guide us,
To love us, whatever we do,
With a warm understanding and infinite patience.

The heart of a mother is full of forgiveness
For any mistake, big or small,
And generous always in helping her family,
Whose needs she has placed above all.

A mother possesses incredible wisdom
And wonderful insight and skill.

Thank you, Moms, for all you do and have done!

Happy Mother's Day!

W.G. Williams

To Be Six Again

4/22/2009

A man was sitting on the edge of the bed observing his wife looking at herself in the mirror. Since her birthday was not far off, he asked what she'd like to have for her birthday.

"I'd like to be six again," she replied, still looking in the mirror.

On the morning of her birthday, he arose early, made her a nice big bowl of Lucky Charms, and then took her to Six Flags theme park. What a day! He put her on every ride in the park; the Death Slide, the Wall of Fear, the Screaming Monster Roller Coaster, everything there was.

Five hours later they staggered out of the theme park. Her head was reeling, and her stomach felt upside down.

He then took her to a McDonald's where he ordered her a Happy Meal with extra fries and a chocolate shake.

Then it was off to a movie, popcorn, a soda pop, and her favorite candy, M&M's. What a fabulous adventure!

Finally she wobbled home with her husband and collapsed into bed exhausted.

He leaned over his wife with a big smile and lovingly asked, "Well Dear, what was it like being six again?"

Her eyes slowly opened and her expression suddenly changed. "I meant my dress size, you retard!"

The moral of the story: ***Even when a man is listening, he's gonna get it wrong.***

Contributed by Jim Haile

Top 10 Myths About Thanksgiving

11/25/2009

MYTH # 1
The Pilgrims Held the First Thanksgiving

To see what the first Thanksgiving was like you have to go to Texas. Texans claim the first Thanksgiving in America actually took place in little San Elizario, a community near El Paso, in 1598 — twenty-three years before the Pilgrims' festival. For several years they have staged a reenactment of the event that culminated in the Thanksgiving celebration: the arrival of Spanish explorer Juan de Onate on the banks of the Rio Grande. De Onate is said to have held a big Thanksgiving festival after leading hundreds of settlers on a grueling 350-mile-long trek across the Mexican desert.

Then again, you may want to go to Virginia. At the Berkeley Plantation on the James River, they claim the first Thanksgiving in America was held there on December 4th, 1619.... two years before the Pilgrims' festival....and every year since 1958 they have reenacted the event. In their view it's not the Mayflower we should remember, it's the Margaret, the little ship which brought 38 English settlers to the plantation in 1619. The story is that the settlers had been ordered by the London company that sponsored them to commemorate the ship's arrival with an annual day of Thanksgiving. Hardly anybody outside Virginia has ever heard of this Thanksgiving, but in 1963 President Kennedy officially recognized the plantation's claim.

But further north in Canada, even 20 years earlier than Texas in 1578, explorer Martin Frobisher had a Thanksgiving for arriving safely in what is now Nunavut!

MYTH # 2
Thanksgiving Was About Family

If by Thanksgiving, you have in mind the Pilgrim festival, forget about it being a family holiday. Put away your Norman Rockwell paintings. Turn off Bing Crosby. Thanksgiving was a multicultural community event. If it had been about family, the Pilgrims never would have invited the Indians to join them.

MYTH # 3
Thanksgiving Was About Religion

No, it wasn't. Paraphrasing the answer provided above, if Thanksgiving had been about religion, the Pilgrims never would have invited the Indians to join them. Besides, the Pilgrims would never have tolerated festivities at a true religious event. Indeed, what we think of as Thanksgiving was really a harvest festival. Actual "Thanksgivings" were religious affairs; everybody spent the day praying. Incidentally, these Pilgrim Thanksgivings occurred at different times of the year, not just in November.

MYTH # 4
The Pilgrims Ate Turkey

What did the Pilgrims eat at their Thanksgiving festival? They didn't have corn on the cob, apples, pears, potatoes or even cranberries. No one knows if they had turkey, although they were used to eating turkey. The only food we know they had for sure was deer. (And they didn't eat with a fork; they didn't have forks back then.)

So how did we get the idea that you have turkey and cranberry and such on Thanksgiving? It was because the Victorians prepared Thanksgiving that way. And they're the ones who made Thanksgiving a national holiday, beginning in 1863, when Abe Lincoln issued his presidential Thanksgiving proclamations…two of them: one to celebrate Thanksgiving in August, a second one in November. Before Lincoln, Americans outside New England did not usually celebrate the holiday. (The Pilgrims, incidentally, didn't become part of the holiday until late in the nineteenth century. Until then, Thanksgiving was simply a day of thanks, not a day to remember the Pilgrims.)

MYTH # 5
The Pilgrims Landed on Plymouth Rock

According to historian George Willison, who devoted his life to the subject, the story about the rock is all malarkey, a public relations stunt pulled off by townsfolk to attract attention. What Willison found out is that the Plymouth Rock legend rests entirely on the dubious testimony of Thomas Faunce, a ninety-five-year-old man, who told the story more than a century after the Mayflower landed. Unfortunately, not too many people ever heard how we came by the story of Plymouth Rock. Willison's book came out at the end of World War II and Americans had more on their minds than Pilgrims then. So, we've all just gone merrily along repeating the same old story as if it's true when it's not. And anyway, the Pilgrims didn't land in Plymouth first. They first made landfall at Provincetown. Of course, the people of Plymouth stick by hoary tradition. Tour guides insist that Plymouth Rock is THE rock.

MYTH # 6
Pilgrims Lived in Log Cabins

No Pilgrim ever lived in a log cabin. The log cabin did not appear in America until late in the seventeenth century, when it was introduced by Germans and Swedes. The very term "log cabin" cannot be found in print until the 1770s. Log cabins were virtually unknown in England at the time the Pilgrims arrived in America. So, what kind of dwellings did the Pilgrims inhabit? As you can see if you visit Plimoth Plantation in Massachusetts, the Pilgrims lived in wood clapboard houses made from sawed lumber.

MYTH # 7
Pilgrims Dressed in Black

Not only did they not dress in black, but they also did not wear those funny buckles, weird shoes, or black steeple hats. So how did we get the idea of the buckles? Plimoth Plantation historian James W. Baker explains that in the nineteenth century, when the popular image of the Pilgrims was formed, buckles served as a kind of emblem of quaintness. That's the reason illustrators gave Santa buckles. Even the blunderbuss, with which Pilgrims are identified, was a symbol of quaintness. The blunderbuss was mainly used to control crowds. It wasn't a hunting rifle. But it looks out of date and fits the Pilgrim stereotype.

MYTH # 8
Pilgrims, Puritans — Same Thing

Though even presidents get this wrong — Ronald Reagan once referred to Puritan John Winthrop as a Pilgrim — Pilgrims and Puritans were two different groups. The Pilgrims came over on the Mayflower and lived in Plymouth. The Puritans, arriving a decade later, settled in Boston. The Pilgrims welcomed heterogeneousness. Some (so-called "strangers") came to America in search of riches, others (so-called "saints") came for religious reasons. The Puritans, in contrast, came over to America strictly in search of religious freedom. Or, to be technically correct, they came over in order to be able to practice their religion freely. They did not welcome dissent. That we confuse Pilgrims and Puritans would have horrified both. Puritans considered the Pilgrims incurable utopians. While both shared the belief that the Church of England had become corrupt, only the Pilgrims believed it was beyond redemption. They therefore chose the path of Separatism. Puritans held out the hope the church would reform.

MYTH # 9
Puritans Hated Sex

Actually, they welcomed sex as a God-given responsibility. When one member of the First Church of Boston refused to have conjugal relations with his wife two years running, he was expelled. Cotton Mather, the celebrated Puritan minister, condemned a married couple who had abstained from sex in order to achieve a higher spirituality. They were the victims, he wrote, of a "blind zeal."

MYTH # 10
Puritans Hated Fun

H.L. Mencken defined Puritanism as "the haunting fear that someone, somewhere, may be happy!" Actually, the Puritans welcomed laughter and dressed in bright colors (or, to be precise, the middle and upper classes dressed in bright colors; members of the lower classes were not permitted to indulge themselves — they dressed in dark clothes). As Carl Degler long ago observed, "The Sabbatarian, antiliquor, and antisex attitudes usually attributed to the Puritans are a nineteenth-century addition to the much more moderate and wholesome view of life's evils held by the early settlers of New England."

W.G. Williams

Train of Life

2/11/2019

At birth we boarded the train and met our parents,
and we believe they will always travel on our side.
However, at some station
our parents will step down from the train,
leaving us on this journey alone.

As time goes by,
other people will board the train;
and they will be significant
i.e. our siblings, friends, children,
and even the love of your life.
Many will step down
and leave a permanent vacuum.
Others will go so unnoticed
that we don't realize
they vacated their seats.

This train ride will be full of joy,
sorrow, fantasy, expectations,
hellos, goodbyes, and farewells.
Success consists of having a good relationship
with all passengers
requiring that we give the best of ourselves.

The mystery to everyone is:
We do not know at which station

we ourselves will step down.
So, we must live in the best way,
love, forgive, and offer the best of who we are.

It is important to do
this because when the time comes for us to step down
and leave our seat empty
we should leave behind beautiful memories
for those who will continue to travel on the train of life.

I wish you a joyful journey on the train of life.
Reap success and give lots of love.
More importantly, thank God for the journey.
Lastly, I thank you
for being one of the passengers on my train.

**(By the way, I am not planning to get off the train anytime soon
but if I do, just remember I am glad you were part of my journey.)**

From Richard Sandford

A Trip to Wal-Mart

7/14/2007

OK! It's the weekend. You're in the middle of some kind of project around the house. Mowing the lawn, putting a new fence in, painting the living room, or whatever. You're hot and sweaty. Covered in dirt or paint. You have your old work clothes on..you know the outfit, shorts with the hole in crotch, old t-shirt with a stain from who knows what, and an old pair of tennis shoes. Suddenly, you realize you need to run to Wal-Mart to get something to help complete the job. Depending on your age you might do the following:

In your 20's:

Stop what you're doing. Shave, take a shower, blow dry your hair, brush your teeth, floss, and put on clean clothes. Check yourself in the mirror and flex. Add a dab of your favorite cologne because you never know, while standing in the checkout lane you just might meet some hot chick you went to school with or the pretty girl running the register.

In your 30's:

Stop what you're doing, put on clean shorts and shirt. Change shoes. You married the hot chick so no need for much else. Wash your hands and comb your hair. Check yourself in the mirror. Still got it. Add a shot of your favorite cologne to cover the smell. The cute girl running the register is the kid sister to someone you went to school with.

In your 40's:

Stop what you're doing. Put a sweatshirt that is long enough to cover the hole in the crotch of your shorts. Put on different shoes and a hat. Wash your hands. Your bottle of Brute Cologne is almost empty so you don't want to waste any of it on a trip to Wal-Mart. Check yourself in the mirror and do more sucking in than flexing. The spicy young thing running the register is your daughter's age and you feel weird thinking she is spicy.

In your 50's:

Stop what you're doing. Put a hat on, wipe the dirt off your hands onto your shirt. Change shoes because you don't want to get dirt in your new sports car. Check yourself in the mirror and you swear not to wear that shirt anymore because it makes you look fat. The cutie running the register smiles when she sees you coming, and you think you still have it. Then you remember the hat you have on is from your buddy's bait shop and it says, "I Got Worms."

In your 60's:

Stop what you're doing. No need for a hat anymore. Hose off the dog crap off your shoes. The mirror was shattered when you were in your 50's. You hope you have underwear on so nothing hangs out the hole in your pants. The girl running the register may be cute but you don't have your glasses on so you are not sure.

In your 70's:

Stop what you're doing. Wait to go to Wal-Mart until they have your prescriptions ready too. Don't' even notice the dog crap on your shoes. The young thing at the register smiles at you because you remind her of her grandfather.

In your 80's:

Stop what you're doing. Start again. Then stop again. Now you remember that you needed to go to Wal-Mart. Go to Wal-Mart and wonder around trying to think what it is you are looking for. Fart out loud and you think someone called out your name. The old lady that greeted you at the front door went to school with you.

In your 90's:

Stop what you are doing.

Contributed by Julius Graw

Unexpected Surgery

5/23/2006

A young boy of six was going into the hospital to have his tonsils removed. He told his playmate, "I'll be gone for a while. I have to have surgery."

On the day he was admitted, his mother asked, "Doctor, my son hasn't been circumcised, would you please do that while he is asleep?"

The doctor agreed.

The boy woke up and was very sore "down there" for several days.

After about a week he got to see his playmate again. The playmate informed him that he was also going to have to have his tonsils out. He asked his friend to tell him about the surgery.

The little boy replied, "All I can tell you is that your tonsils ain't where you think they are."

Contributed by David Taylor

Vodka Christmas Cake

12/20/2022

Once again this year, I've had requests for my Vodka Christmas Cake recipe so here goes. Please keep in your files as I'm beginning to get tired of typing this up every year! (I made mine this morning!!!!)

    1 cup sugar,
    1 tsp. baking powder,
    1 cup water,
    1 tsp. salt ,
    1 cup brown sugar,
    1 tsp Lemon juice,
    4 large eggs,
    Nuts,
    1 bottle Vodka,
    2 cups dried fruit.

Sample a cup of Vodka to check quality. Take a large bowl, check the Vodka again to be sure it is of the highest quality then Repeat.

Turn on the electric mixer. Beat one cup of butter in a large fluffy bowl. Add 1 teaspoon of sugar. Beat again.

At this point, it is best to make sure the Vodka is at correct temperature, so another cup just in case.

Turn off the mixer thingy.

Break 2 eggs and add to the bowl and chuck in the cup of fried druit.

Pick the fruit up off the floor, wash it and put it in the bowl a piece at a time trying to count it.

Mix on the turner. If the fried fruit gets stuck in the beaters, just pry it loose with a drewsriver

Sample the Vodka to test for condentricity.

Next, sift 2 cups of salt, or something.

Check the Vodka.

Add one table, a poon of spugar, or suom fink.

Whativer you can find.

Greace the oven.

Turn the cake tin 630 degrees and try not to fall over.

Don't forget to beat off the turner. Finly, throw the bowl fruh the winder.

Finish the Vodka and wipe the counter with the cat.

Contributed by Julius Graw

Ways the Bible Would be Different

(If Written by College Students)
8/23/2007

10. The Last Supper would have been eaten the next morning - cold.
9. The Ten Commandments are actually only five, double-spaced, and written in a large font.
8. There would be a new edition every two years in order to limit reselling.
7. Any forbidden fruit would have been eaten because it wasn't cafeteria food.
6. Paul's letter to the Romans becomes Paul's e-mail to <u>abuse@romans.gov</u>.
5. Reason Cain killed Abel -- They were roommates.
4. The place where the end of the world occurs -- Finals, not Armageddon.
3. Out go the mules, in come the mountain bikes.
2. Reason why Moses and followers walked in desert for 40 years -- They didn't want to ask directions and look like freshmen.
1. Instead of God creating the world in six days and resting on the seventh, He would have put it off until the night before it was due and then pulled an all-nighter.

Contributed by Tom Benner

Wednesday's Smiles

5/1/2024

"Found this sign in front of someone's home (Canada)"
WARNING
Retired person
on the premises.
Knows everything
and has plenty of
time to tell it.

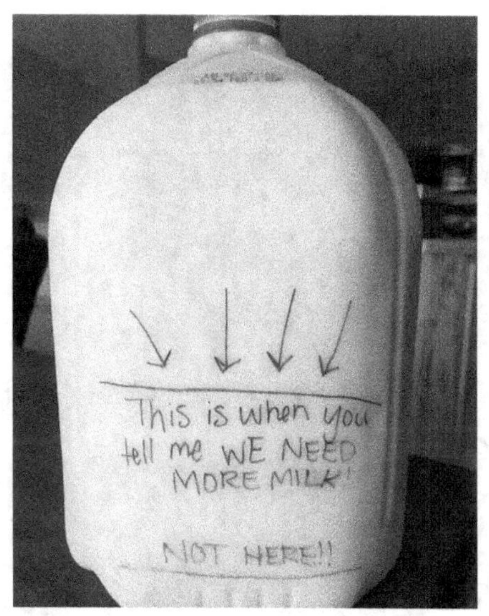
This is when you
tell me WE NEED
MORE MILK!
NOT HERE!!

Calling twin brother from prison

I don't know if Facebook has ever caused the lame to walk but it has sure caused the dumb to speak.

Having a teenage daughter is like having a cat that only comes out to eat and hisses when you try and be nice to it.

Get a baby gate they said, it'll keep them safe it said....

Most people are at the age where they are using their phones to document the good times in their lives. I'm at the age where I use my phone to take pictures of labels that I can't read and use my phone to enlarge the print so that I can read it.

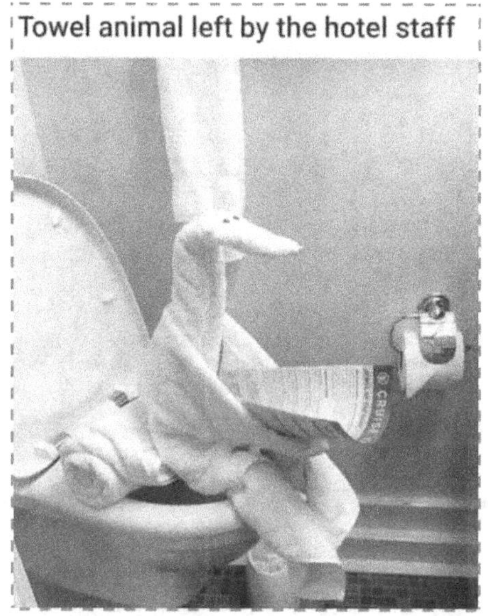

Towel animal left by the hotel staff

Apparently there are
2 types of flu.
The harmless one that
women and children get,
and the "near death"
version that men get.

Restaurant bills are designed to be paid by men, that is why it is called men-u
You're wrong, it's actually me-n-u

Why must I prove
that I am me to pay my
bills over the phone?
Do strangers call to
pay my Bills? And if
they do, why don't
you let them?

Condolences and Funnies

If Only
Vegetables
Smelt As
Good As Bacon

I TOLD YOU I WAS SICK

IF YOUR DOG
POOPS
PICK IT UP
PLEASE

Americans: We walked on the moon

Also Americans:

[Open box before eating pizza.]

Contributed by Bernard and Jean Scott

What Is Sex?

5/6/2009

An out-of-breath seven-year-old girl ran up to her grandfather, who was tinkering in his workshop, and confronted him with the universally dreaded question: "What is sex...?"

He was surprised she'd ask such a question at her age but, he thought, if she's old enough to ask, she's old enough to get a straight answer. He wouldn't shirk his responsibilities.

Steeling himself to leave nothing out, he proceeded to describe for her all the variations of human sexuality he could conjure, careful to impress upon her the joys and responsibilities of intercourse and procreation.

When finally, Grandpa was done pontificating, the little girl stood frozen, as though nailed to the spot, and looked at him with her mouth open, eyes wide in amazement.

Seeing she was overwhelmed, he asked what caused her sudden curiosity.

His granddaughter shook off her reverie and replied, "Grandma says dinner will be ready in a couple of secs."

Contributed by Ron Gargasz

What Teachers Make

10/9/2006

The dinner guests were sitting around the table discussing life. One man, a CEO, decided to explain the problem with education. He argued, "What is a kid going to learn from someone who decided his best option in life was to become a teacher?" He then reminded the other dinner guests of what they say about teachers: "Those who can, do. Those who can't, teach."

To emphasize his point, he said to another guest, "You're a teacher, Susan. Be honest. What do you make?"

Susan, who had a reputation for honesty and frankness replied, "You want to know what I make?

* "I make kids work harder than they ever thought they could.
* "I make a C+ feel like the winner of the Congressional Medal of Honor.
* "I make kids sit through 40 minutes of study hall in absolute silence.
* "You want to know what I make?
* "I make kids wonder.
* "I make them question.
* "I make them criticize.
* "I make them apologize and mean it.
* "I make them write.
* "I make them read, read, read.
* "I make them show all their work in math and perfect their final drafts in English. I make them understand that if you have the brains, and follow your heart, and if someone ever tries

to judge you by what you make, you must pay no attention because they just didn't learn."

Susan paused and then continued. "You want to know what I make? I MAKE A DIFFERENCE.
What do YOU make?"

Contributed by Bonnie & Bubba Mehling

Wisdom Comes with Age

1/10/2019

I can *explain* it to you..
But I can't *understand* it for you!

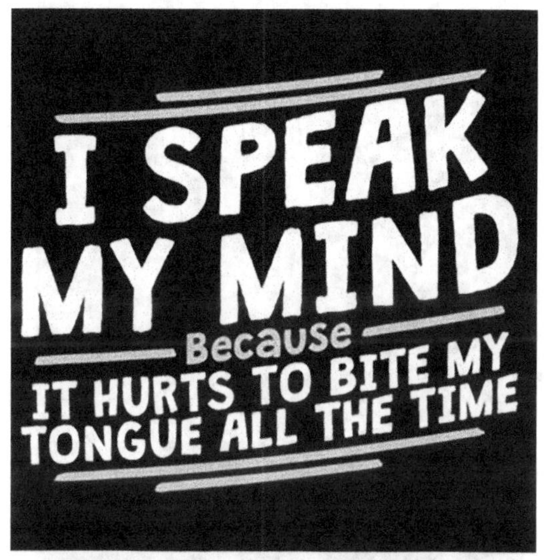

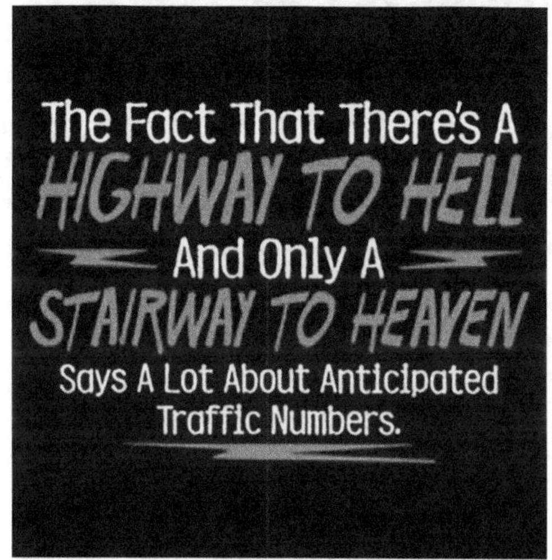

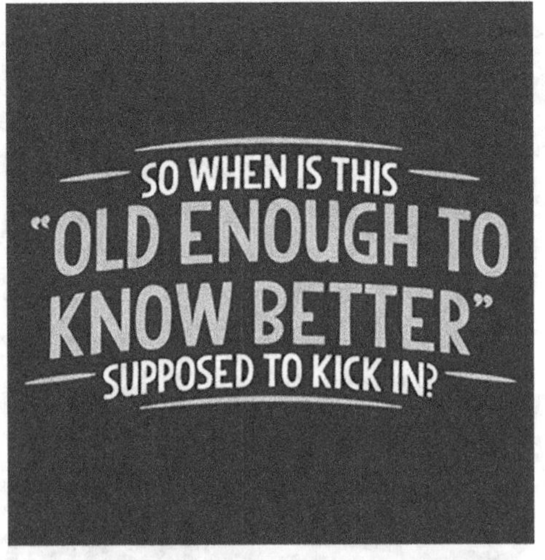
SO WHEN IS THIS
"OLD ENOUGH TO
KNOW BETTER"
SUPPOSED TO KICK IN?

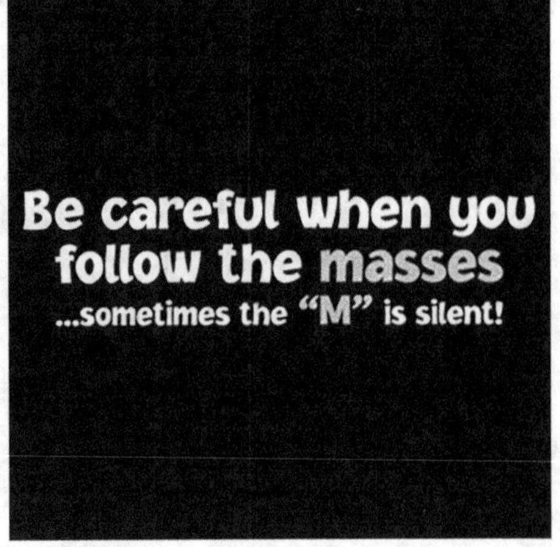
Be careful when you
follow the masses
...sometimes the "M" is silent!

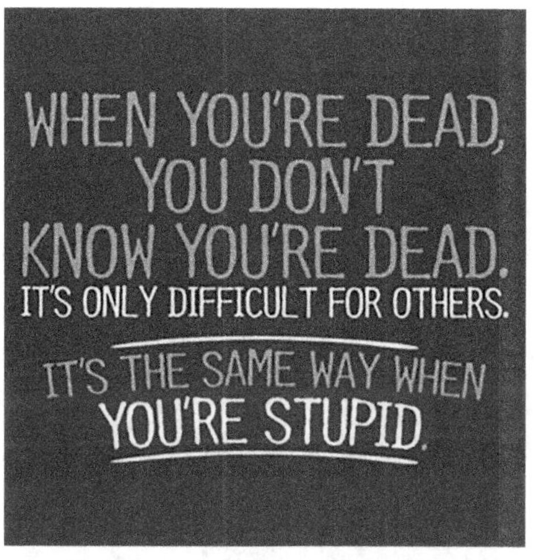

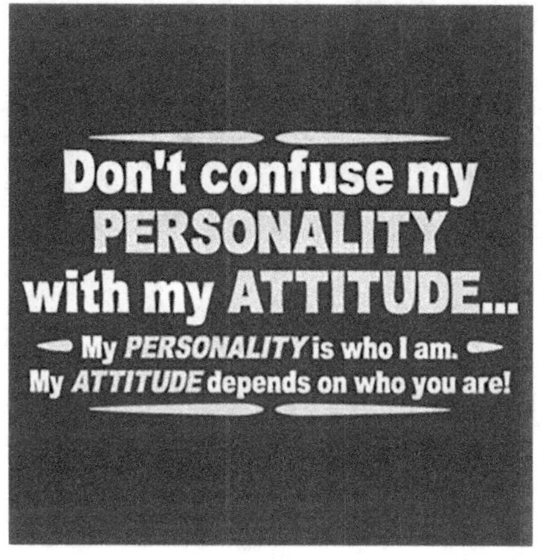

Don't worry about old age…it won't last very long

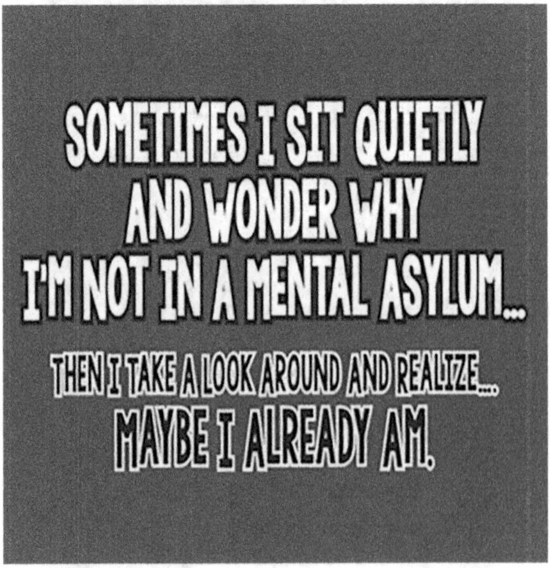

From Sharon Buckholtz

Wordplay to Make Your Day

3/11/2006

- If you don't pay your exorcist, you get repossessed.
- With her marriage, she got a new name and a dress.
- Show me a piano falling down a mine shaft, and I'll show you A flat minor.
- When a clock is hungry, it goes back four seconds.
- The man who fell into an upholstery machine is fully recovered.
- A grenade thrown into a kitchen in France would result in Linoleum Blownapart.
- You feel stuck with your debt if you can't budge it.
- Local Area Network in Australia: The LAN down under.
- He often broke into song because he couldn't find the key.
- Every calendar's days are numbered.
- A lot of money is tainted. It t'aint yours and it t'aint mine.
- A boiled egg in the morning is hard to beat.
- He had a photographic memory that was never developed.
- The short fortuneteller who escaped from prison was a small medium at large.
- Once you've seen one shopping center you've seen a mall.
- Those who jump off a Paris bridge are in Seine.
- When an actress saw her first strands of gray hair, she thought she'd dye.
- Bakers trade bread recipes on a knead-to-know basis.
- Santa's helpers are subordinate clauses.
- Acupuncture is a jab well done.

Contributed by Jim Phillips

Words

8/23/2023

A truck loaded with thousands of copies of Roget's Thesaurus crashed yesterday losing its entire load. Witnesses were stunned, startled, aghast, taken aback, stupefied, confused, shocked, rattled, paralyzed, dazed, bewildered, mixed up, surprised, awed, dumbfounded, nonplussed, flabbergasted, astounded, amazed, confounded, astonished, overwhelmed, horrified, numbed, speechless and perplexed.

Meanwhile, those waiting for the shipment were at a loss for words.

Contributed by Debbie Papay

Worth Sharing

10/15/2024

I recently asked a dear friend, who is in his 70s nearing 80, about the changes he's noticed in himself as he's grown older. His response was so beautiful, I just had to share it with you:

1. After spending a lifetime loving my parents, siblings, spouse, children, and friends - I've finally started loving myself.
2. I've realized that I am not "Atlas." The world doesn't rest on my shoulders.
3. I no longer haggle with vegetable or fruit vendors. A few extra pennies won't hurt me, but it might help them save for their daughter's school fees.
4. I always leave my waitress a generous tip. That little extra might bring a smile to her face as she works hard for her living.
5. I've stopped telling the elderly that they've already repeated that story. It allows them to relive their precious memories.
6. I no longer feel the need to correct people, even when I know they're wrong. It's not my job to make everyone perfect - peace is far more valuable than perfection.
7. I freely give compliments. They lift the mood of both the giver and receiver. And remember, if you receive one, never turn it down - just say "Thank you."
8. A crease or spot on my shirt? I don't sweat it anymore. Personality speaks louder than appearances.
9. I've learned to walk away from people who don't value me. They may not know my worth, but I do.

10. I stay calm when others try to outrun me in life's rat race. I am not a rat, and I'm not racing.
11. I'm no longer embarrassed by my emotions - they're what make me human.
12. I've learned that it's better to drop the ego than to break a relationship. Ego isolates, but relationships keep you connected.
13. I live each day as if it could be my last, because one day, it will be.
14. And lastly, I'm doing what makes me happy. I'm responsible for my happiness, and happiness is a choice you can make at any moment.

Why wait until we're 60, 70, or 80 to start living this way? Let's practice these lessons now, at any age.
This insightful message was shared by a wise friend, and I'm simply passing along his words of wisdom.

Contributed by Steve Overholt

You Know You Live on the Gulf Coast After Katrina When...

10/01/2005

You have FEMA's number on your speed dialer.

You have more than 300 C and D batteries in your kitchen drawer.

Your pantry contains more than 20 cans of Spaghetti-Os.

You're thinking of repainting your house to match
the plywood covering your windows.

When describing your house to a prospective buyer, you say
it has three bedrooms, two baths and one safe hallway.

Your SSN isn't a secret, it's written in Sharpie on your arms.

You're on a first-name basis with the cashier at Home Depot.

You're delighted to pay only $3 for a gallon of regular unleaded.

The road leading to your house has been declared a No-Wake Zone.

You decide that your patio furniture looks
better on the bottom of the pool.

You own more than three large coolers.

You can wish that other people get hit by a hurricane
and not feel the least bit guilty about it.

You rationalize helping a friend board up by thinking
"It'll only take gallon of gas to get there and back"

You have 2-liter coke bottles and milk jugs
filled with water in your freezer.

Three months ago you couldn't hang a shower curtain; today
you can assemble a portable generator by candlelight.

You catch a 13-pound redfish. In your driveway.

You can recite from memory whole portions of
your homeowner's insurance policy.

You consider a "vacation" to stunning Tupelo, Mississippi.

At cocktail parties, women are attracted to
the guy with the biggest chainsaw.

You have had tuna fish more than 5 days in a row.

There's a roll of tar paper in your garage.

You can rattle off the names of three or more
meteorologists who work at the Weather Channel.

Ice is a valid topic of conversation.

Your "drive-thru" meal consists of MRE's and bottled water.

Relocating to South Dakota does not seem like such a crazy idea.

You spend more time on your roof then in your living room.

You've been laughed at over the phone by a
roofer, fence builder or a tree worker.

A battery powered TV is considered a home entertainment center.

You don't worry about relatives wanting to visit during the summer.

Your child's first words are "hunker down"
and you didn't go to Ole Miss!

Having a tree in your living room does not
necessarily mean it's Christmas.

Toilet Paper is elevated to coin of the realm at shelters.

You know the difference between the "good
side" and the "bad side" of a storm.

You go to work early and stay late just to enjoy the air conditioning.

Contributed by Les Skinner

Contributors

Abke, Gary
Anderson, Linda
Ascunce, Raul
Benner, Tom
Bialecki, Dennis
Buckholtz, Sharon
Butler, Tim
Butler, Tod
Cowan, Barbara
D'Antonio, Bill
Flahiff, Judy
Gargasz, Ron
Gillett, Jamie
Graw, Julius
Greenwood, Jim
Haile, Jim
Hallford, E.W.
Heisler, Dawn
Heisler, Ron
Hoiles, David
Hunt, John
Luna, Susan

Mehling, Bubba
Mehling, Bonnie
Narges, Linda
Niese, Sherry
O'Dell, Donald
Overholt, Steve
Papay, Debby
Phillips, Jim
Sandford, Richard
Schroeder, Fred
Scott, Bernard and Jean
Silveman, David A.
Skinner, Les
Taylor, David
Teague, Wells
Thornton, Gary
Williams, W.G.
Wonderly, Barbara

In Memoriam

This is one of the most difficult pieces to write as I remember the contributors who have passed away. **Ron and Dawn Heisler, E.W. Hallford, Fred Schroeder, David Taylor** and **Bubba and Bonnie Mehling** were all mentioned in Volume Two.

But Volume Three brings more passings. I encountered an internet post that **Tom Benner** had passed away a few years ago and I had not heard at the time. Tom had been one of my most frequent contributors in the early years and, unfortunately, we had never actually met.

Another friend who will be missed is **Bill D'Antonio**, a friend from my years in Washington, DC where he was a professor at the Catholic University of America.

Finally, **David Hoiles**, a client of almost two decades passed away earlier this year.

All of these folks have left great "Thoughts" that will keep them in our memories for years!

Author's Notes

I've been sending out a "Thought for the Day" for more than three decades now, and what began as a simple attempt to keep in touch with a few salespeople has grown into a global circle of readers who value reflection, encouragement, and a shared moment to pause in a busy world.

Over the years, these Thoughts have been shaped not just by my own experiences but by the wisdom, humor and insight generously offered by friends, readers, mentors, and countless voices who've inspired me along the way. I continue to be humbled by how many people contribute stories, ideas, and perspectives that ultimately find their way into these daily messages.

As this tradition evolves, so do the lessons it teaches me – about gratitude, curiosity, resilience, and the quiet power of connection. My hope is that each day's Thought brings readers a spark of perspective or comfort, just as preparing them has brought meaning and joy into my life.

The community that has grown around these daily reflections remains one of my greatest privileges. And as always, I happily welcome anyone who would like to join us on this continuing journey of thoughtful encouragement. Simply send me a note at bill@internet-humor.com and I'll start your "Thought for the Day." No cost!

W.G. (Bill) Williams

Twenty Years of Laughter, One Email at a Time

What happens when you send a daily humor email to thousands of people for more than two decades? You create a time capsule of laughter, nostalgia, and humanity.

Volume Three continues the beloved "20 Years of Internet Humor" series with even more unforgettable moments—from hilarious court transcripts to children's interpretations of the Bible, from observations about small-town America to reflections on life, faith, and family.

Whether you're reliving the dial-up internet era or discovering these stories for the first time, Volume Three delivers the perfect blend of humor and heart.

What Readers Are Saying:

★ ★ ★ ★ ★ "I really enjoyed it, laughing out loud again and again. A perfect companion on a commute, or for those minutes waiting at the dentist." — Lucinda E Clarke, Readers' Favorite

★ ★ ★ ★ ★ "A delightful and revealing collection of internet humor spanning two decades." — Readers' Favorite

★ ★ ★ ★ ★ "Endorsed by Jack Canfield, co-author of Chicken Soup for the Soul"

Perfect For: Coffee tables • Gift-giving • Bedside reading • Bathroom humor (yes, really!)

Open to any page. Read for 2-3 minutes. Smile. Repeat tomorrow.

🎁 BONUS: Scan the QR code for early access to Volume Four + exclusive reader content!